HAUNTED
NORTH
CAROLINA
COAST

HAUNTED NORTH CAROLINA COAST

THOMAS SMITH

Haunted America

Published by Haunted America
A Division of The History Press
Charleston, SC
www.historypress.com

Bodie Island Lighthouse. © *Haysues23, Robert Ranson Photography*.

First published 2024

Manufactured in the United States

ISBN 9781467158169

Library of Congress Control Number: 2024936749

DEDICATION

Most writers I know dedicate their books to someone they know or maybe someone who had a major influence on them during their lifetime. I've done that. Most, if not all, of my writer friends and acquaintances have done it. But I think, this time, I want to do things a little differently. I want to dedicate this book to the people who normally don't see their names in book dedications.

So, if you have ever told ghost stories around a campfire, read scary stories under a blanket with a flashlight or braved ghosts anywhere else in the dark; if you have ever said something like, "Hey, be careful around the old Simmons place. They say it's haunted"; if you have ever looked out to sea and scanned the horizon because this just might be the night the haunted pirate ship makes its appearance; or if you have ever been in a place that suddenly made the hair stand up on the back of your neck and goosebumps pop up on your arms, then this book is dedicated to you. Also, if you just picked this book up off the rack and said, "This looks interesting, I think I'll give it a shot," that's good enough for me. This book is dedicated to you, too—with my thanks.

And as always, this one is for Melanie. Not every wife could walk by a room and hear the "You know, you're right. We really do need a headless specter in the second section," part of a conversation and not even break her stride or hear her husband say to an editor on the phone, "Yeah, the novella is just about finished. I just need to figure out what round a Weatherby Mark V would take to obliterate a vampire's heart and blow his brains out in only two shots," without making me sleep on the porch.

In the meanwhile you shall understand that, since Sir Richard Greenville's departure from us, as also before, we have discovered the main to be the goodliest soil under the cope of heaven, so abounding with sweet trees, that bring such sundry rich and pleasant gums, grapes of such greatness, yet wild, as Spain, France, nor Italy have no greater.

—an extract of Master Ralph Laine's letter to M. Richard Hakluyt on September 3, 1545, describing coastal North Carolina

Ye who, passing graves by night,
Glance not to the left nor right,
Lest a spirit should arise,
Cold and white, to freeze your eyes.

—James Russell Lowell, "The Ghost-Seer"

CONTENTS

CONTENTS

ACKNOWLEDGEMENTS

Thank you to Mary Ames Booker, a curator with the Battleship North Carolina, for helping me access pictures and some valuable information.

A big thank-you to Nelson Nauss, the executive director/founder of the Ghost Guild, for going above and beyond the call of duty when it came to helping me find photographs and information. He and his group are consummate professionals who consult with some of the most well-known entities (no pun intended) in the state.

Thank you to Cyndi Brown, a public information officer for the N.C. Maritime Museums, who helped me access photographs and gave me some really excellent suggestions.

I also want to thank Al Parker, the author of the Ghosts, Legends, and Lore of Historic Murfreesboro tour, and Ami Wilson, the executive director of the Murfreesboro Historical Association. My section on Murfreesboro only scratches the surface of just how haunted that town really is. You could fill a book with information on Murfreesboro alone. In fact, I'm sure the historical association will be more than happy to send you on the full tour—if you're not afraid.

Thank you to Ashley Hill and the staff at The History Press for making this project possible. Books like this are one of the reasons I wanted to become a writer in the first place.

And the biggest thank-you of all goes to my editor, Kate Jenkins, who worked with me and encouraged me through heart valve replacement surgery and recovery, two funerals and life generally turning itself inside out for a while. She is a big reason you are holding this book in your hands right now. And if there's a Super Editor Award out there somewhere, I'm going to make sure her name is at the top of the nominations list.

PART I

WHY IS THE NORTH CAROLINA COAST SO HAUNTED?

Many places are said to be haunted, houses, inns, forts, hospitals, asylums and graveyards—definitely graveyards. Any place where tragedy strikes or any place where a terrible injustice has been perpetrated has the potential to become haunted. But how can an *entire region* like the North Carolina Coast come to be known as haunted? Well, that's the question, isn't it? And the primary reason is that the coast of the Tarheel State has an abundance of places where tragedy occurred or death has visited and decided to stay. These locations can be found in almost every hamlet and village in the area. But it hasn't always been that way. In a letter to Richard Hakluyt on September 3, 1585, Ralph Laine referred to North Carolina as "the goodliest soil under the cope of heaven." Basically, the state was considered a paradise on Earth.

But time passed and things began to happen, tragic things, dark things, unexplained things, things that defied explanation. And as the centuries passed, the state garnered another, slightly more sinister designation: it became one of the most haunted places on Earth, particularly its coastal area. Take the Outer Banks for example. Ocracoke has long been called the most haunted place in North Carolina. (Not bad for an island that's just 9.6 miles long.) Then again, Ocracoke was primed to be a hotbed of ghostly sightings and supernatural activity, because in that relatively short stretch of land, there are eighty-three cemeteries. And that doesn't include the unmarked graves of pirates, shipwrecked sailors and enslaved people on the island.

Public cemeteries, family cemeteries and military cemeteries abound. As a case in point, there are four British Royal Navy sailors buried in the Ocracoke British Cemetery. Theirs were the only bodies recovered after their ship went down just off the coast of Ocracoke. As the story is told, in the early days of World War II, the waters along the North Carolina coast were referred to as "Torpedo Alley," because the German submarines, always prowling that portion of the coast during the war, sank almost four hundred ships in that area. On May 11, 1942, while on patrol off the coast of North Carolina, the HMT *Bedfordshire* was torpedoed by a German submarine. When the smoke cleared, all thirty-seven of the British sailors onboard were found to have been killed, but only four of the bodies washed ashore. The rest were never recovered. Do their spirits haunt the ocean where they died? Are they restless spirits? Nobody really knows. But the four British sailors who rest on the island rest in peace.

Even so, other cemeteries on Ocracoke are not so tranquil. Take the community cemetery in Sunset Village for example. On more than one occasion, an elderly couple dressed in nineteenth-century clothes have been seen there. And then there's the case of Fannie Pearl McWilliams Wahab. Her grave (located in a different part of the island) is marked with a "No Trespassing" sign in an effort to deter people from trying to recreate their own paranormal experience at her final resting place. And that brings up an interesting question: Why would someone think Fannie's grave could be the key to a paranormal experience? Ah, that would be telling. Her story *is*, however, in this book. But it raises more questions than it answers. And hers is one story best read with the lights on. And here's a reminder: supernatural events are not limited to cemeteries alone.

But let's get back to our haunted coast. In addition to holding specters in cemeteries, the coast contains places where it's best not to walk at night. Springer's Point Nature Preserve comes to mind. It's beautiful during the day. The preserve is home to a maritime forest, tidal red cedar, a salt marsh, wet grasslands and a sound-front beach. The area is also accessible only by foot or bicycle. Wandering through the preserve is an experience not to be missed—during the day, that is. But at night, things change. Once night falls, it would be best for you to spend your time somewhere

Springer's Point is an ideal place for a leisurely stroll—unless something is chasing you. © *Liz Albro.*

else, because when the sun goes down, there is more out there than nature. Many people have reported seeing a large, bearded ghost on the paths of the reserve. And some unlucky souls have even been chased by the specter.

A former musician, now deceased, recounted for years his experience of observing the large, bearded specter sitting on an abandoned cistern near the grave of Sam Jones. The apparition saw the musician and chased him through the woods, all the way to the sound, where he vanished into smoke. If that's not enough, add to that the fact that Springer's Point was a favorite haunt (no pun intended) of Edward Teach, otherwise known as Blackbeard, and was the site of one of the largest pirate gatherings of his era. Shortly after a multiday party where Blackbeard and his companions cooked a hog, drank, sang and danced, the pirate was captured and beheaded. And no, that wasn't the end of Blackbeard. His beheading was a frightening event in itself, one that made even the boldest of pirates shrink back and wish they were anywhere else. And some say Blackbeard is still there today—minus his head. But more about him later.

So far, we have Ocracoke, with its haunted cemeteries, trails and buildings and at least one pirate searching for his head—and that's just the beginning. As you move away from Ocracoke and make your way down the coast, there is the town of Bath, where a horse race sent one rider straight to hell, and the evidence of that fateful race is still there.

There are ghost ships like the *Carroll A. Deering* and what is most commonly referred to as the Flaming Ship of Ocracoke. And since we are talking about the coast, there are, of course, lighthouses, which are home to ghosts who harbor terrible secrets. In fact, two of those lighthouses share a ghost. There are inns, hotels and bars along the coast, where former patrons return from beyond the grave to wander the hallways, move items, watch living guests and otherwise cling to their previous lives. There are homes where the deceased are still in residence. And these hauntings are not restricted to locations from the distant past. Oh, no. A popular three-star resort hotel, established in the 1970s, has a permanent resident. As the story is told, a guest had a heart attack on the property, and his spirit roams the resort to this day. The apparition, who appears dressed in a gray suit and bowtie, makes the occasional visit but is usually content to just open doors, raise and lower the shades and turn lights on and off.

And one of the coast's most unusual haunted places is not a home or other building; it's a battleship, the USS *North Carolina* to be specific. And while ten sailors died in battle and eight others died in the line of duty on the ship (a relatively small number for a battleship that was actively deployed in a time of war), not all of the honored dead left the ship. Some, for reasons unknown, stayed behind and are still there.

Wilmington, Buxton, Southport, Pasquotank, Ocean Isle and many other coastal towns are home to specters, ghosts, paranormal events and eerie, unexplained occurrences. They are brimming with what the 1926 *Cornish and West Country Litany* refers to as "ghoulies and ghosties and long-leggedy beasties, and things that go bump in the night." And this just scratches the surface. So, why is the coast of North Carolina such a haunted place?

Let me tell you a story…

1

THE HOOFPRINTS AT BATH

"Either take me a winner or take me to hell."

Jesse Elliott was a drinker, a fighter, a gambler and an avid horse racer. In fact, the only thing he liked more than whiskey, brawling and betting, was racing his horse against all comers. Any time, any place, it didn't matter to Jesse. If somebody had a horse and wanted to bet on the outcome of a race, Jesse was ready to ride, even on a Sunday. It didn't matter to him. However, on Sunday, October 13, 1813, Jesse would have done well to heed his wife's admonition and either stay home or go with her to church instead of accepting his last ill-fated challenge.

Jesse's day started in downtown Bath at the Commons, like most of his days. He was talking with a few of his companions and bragging more than usual when a stranger dressed all in black walked up and addressed him by name. Jesse's dog, his constant companion, lowered his head and growled deep in his chest. Jesse tried to quiet the dog, but he continued to growl, his hackles rising. The stranger, tall and severe looking in his black attire, said he had heard of Jesse's reputation as a racer. The stranger said he was certain that he and his horse could beat Jesse in a race. And he issued a challenge to race him: "Jesse, I understand you have a fast horse, but I believe my horse is faster. And although I have also heard about your prowess as a horse racer, I have no doubt I can beat you in a race."

"Well, stranger," Jesse said, winking at his companions, "we'll just see about that. I'll tell you what. If it is agreeable with you, I'll go home and get my horse, then we'll meet back here in one hour, and see who really is the fastest." The stranger thought a moment, smiled an unnerving smile and agreed. With that, Jesse headed home to get his horse.

Jesse blew into his house like a mad whirlwind. Jesse ignored his wife, just as he did on most Sundays when his wife pleaded with him to go to church with her. He just shoved her aside and pulled on his riding boots. "I don't have time for your foolishness today," he said, and then he headed for the pantry where he kept his whisky. He had a few drinks and then headed toward the barn where his horse waited. While he saddled the horse, his dog appeared and started growling again. Jesse told the dog to be quiet, but the dog kept growling, as if in warning. Finally, Jesse mounted his horse and rode back toward town, leaving the agitated dog in his wake.

When he reached the agreed upon location, Jesse was met by the stranger, who was dressed in black and astride the largest, most powerful-looking horse Jesse had ever seen. The stallion was midnight black, and its eyes flashed with an eerie fire. For the first time in his life, Jesse was having second thoughts about accepting a race challenge. But not one to back down from a race, especially with his friends watching, he pulled up even with the stranger, and they agreed on the route the race would take. One of Jesse's friends fired a shot in the air, and the two horses leaped forward in a storm of pounding hooves and flying dirt.

Some say animals have a special sense. What exactly did Jesse Elliott's dog see? What did it know that he didn't? © *Spela Znidarsic.*

Jesse Elliott spurred his horse on, urging his mount for more speed while running the race of his life. Was it a race to hell? © Selena2009.

Jesse pulled ahead of the stranger and spurred his horse harder. His horse responded with an immediate burst of speed, and Jesse pressed his knees into the horse's sides and leaned low over his mount. Even though his steed surged forward, Jesse heard the stranger's horse snorting just a few feet behind him. He heard the thundering hooves pounding the earth, and it seemed he could feel the hot air being exhaled through the mighty stallion's nostrils. Even so, Jesse had the strange feeling that the other rider was holding his horse back. Maybe he was waiting for the proper moment to make his move. But Jesse kept his eyes ahead and urged his horse on with every ounce of speed he could muster. He spurred his horse and leaned over its strong neck. His horse responded, erupting in a burst of speed like never before. Jesse heard his horse take in mighty lungfuls of air and felt its mighty muscles expand and contract in perfect rhythm. And as he streaked toward the finish line, still he heard the stranger's midnight black stallion right behind him. It was as if the stranger was holding the great beast back for some reason yet still matched him stride for stride.

Jesse saw the curve in the road and knew if he could hold his lead just another minute, he would keep his undefeated streak intact. The curve marked the beginning of the last few hundred yards of the race. If he could just hold this breakneck pace, he would defeat the stranger and his powerful horse. With that bit of reassurance in mind, he cried out to his horse, "Either take me a winner or take me to hell!" At that moment, Jesse's horse turned its head to look behind them, its mane flying wildly and foam flying from its mouth with the exertion of keeping ahead of the dark stranger. Jesse's horse whinnied loudly, and whatever it saw behind them made it stop abruptly. It planted all four hooves in the dirt, stopping on the spot. But Jesse's momentum pitched him over the horse's head and headlong into a pine tree. His neck broke on impact, and he was dead before he fell to the ground.

When Jesse's friends arrived at the scene of the accident, there was no stranger and no massive black horse. There were just the hoofprints clearly visible next to the body. Oddly enough, there were five hoofprints instead of four. Some say the fifth hoofprint belongs to the mysterious rider's horse and was planted there when the stranger took Jesse's soul to hell. As the story was told by witnesses to the aftermath of the tragic race, clumps of Jesse's red hair were tangled in the bark of the tree for years. Eventually, that half of the tree died while the other half remained green until it was cut down. Only a stump remains, and the hoofprints are still there—all five. And all attempts to alter or eradicate the hoofprints over the last two hundred years have failed.

2

WHERE ARE YOU, MY SON?

Even death cannot diminish the bond between a mother and her son.

Many years ago, in a dense stand of pines, out where the Neuse River empties into the Pamlico Sound, there stood an old shack. And in that shack lived an old blind woman and her son. Life was hard, and the land was unforgiving. But they managed. The waters near the shack kept them fed, and the boy was able to sell what they didn't use themselves. Fish, crabs and clams were abundant in those days. And the boy also gathered berries, medicinal roots and other things from the surrounding woods. There were also plenty of deer, rabbits, quail and squirrels, all of which kept them fed and helped the boy bring in what little money he could. And while things were difficult at times, they were accustomed to the hardscrabble life, and the two lived in the old cabin together, happy and content.

The woman seldom ventured far from the cabin, but on those occasions when she did, she carried a long stick and tapped it like a cane to help her navigate the uneven terrain. Occasionally, she would go into the yard or as far as the edge of the woods, but she never went into the deep woods, and neither did she try to walk out to the water. She was content to stay near the cabin, always knowing that if she needed anything, her son would hear her call and would come to her immediately.

If she needed help with something in the house, all she had to do was say, "Where are you, my son?" and no matter how softly she called out for him, he would hear her and came to her. If she needed a fire in the hearth, she need only call out, "Where are you, my son?" And soon, he would be there, building a nice, warm fire. If she wanted him to read to her, she would call out, "Where are you, my son?" And before long, he would be by her side, reading to the old woman. No matter where he was or how softly she called, he was so accustomed to listening for her voice that he was able to hear her and come to her.

But one day, a big rain came. The skies opened up, and the rain came down hard and constant. The torrential rains lasted for a week, and the boy was unable to fish, forage in the woods or dig for clams. Hunting was also out of the question. So, he stayed in the cabin with his mother all that week. When the rain finally ended, the boy went out to fish, hunt and gather other bounty from the water, as was his habit. But as he worked along the shoreline, the trip took a tragic turn. Because of the torrential rains, the bank was unstable, and while the boy was setting his fishing net, the bank collapsed and he fell into the water. The old woman's son was a strong swimmer, but because of the constant rain and sheer volume of water, the current, much stronger than usual, swept him away. No matter what he tried, no matter how hard he kicked, he was no match for the surging water. And in the end, the river won. It pulled him down, and the young man drowned.

Later in the day, the boy's mother became cold and called out for him to stoke the fire, but there was no response. At first, she was not alarmed. She knew the muddy conditions would most likely slow him down. But as

The shack stands empty, but in the woods nearby, a mother searches for her son. © *Publicdomainphotos, Dreamstime.com.*

time passed, she became worried and continued to call, "Where are you, my son?" But every time her cry for her son was met with silence, she became more agitated. Then she became worried. This was not like him. When her calls, each more urgent than the last, went unanswered, she became afraid and made the difficult decision to try to find her son.

Her efforts to find her son took a tragic turn, and the old woman's body was found a few weeks later near the river. She had become lost in the woods and died, all the while calling out, "Where are you, my son?" But the story doesn't end there. Long after the cabin had been forgotten, and the old woman and her son were little more than a distant memory, people in the surrounding area reported hearing the sound of tapping and a woman's voice calling, "Where are you, my son?" And years later, shortly after Camp Seagull was built in Arapahoe, North Carolina, around 1948, campers and counselors alike insisted that sometimes, when the camp was dark and everyone was in bed, they could hear the sound of something tapping the ground and a voice calling out in the night, "Where are you, my son?" *Tap…tap…tap.* "Where are you, my son?"

3

NELL CROPSEY

Is Nell Cropsey lingering until justice is served?

What ended as one of the most sensational murder cases in Elizabeth City's history actually had its beginning in an almost idyllic situation. In 1898, William Hardy Cropsey, his wife, Mary Louise Cropsey, and their two daughters, Nell and Olive, made the move from Brooklyn, New York, to Elizabeth City, North Carolina. The newly appointed justice of Pasquotank County and his family made their home on a sixty-five-acre plantation on Riverside Drive, and the future looked bright for the family. The daughters were quite beautiful, and soon, they had a steady stream of suitors vying for their attention.

Their new residence was different from their previous home in Brooklyn, but the family soon settled in and became a valued part of the community. After a while, the two young women were in serious relationships with a couple of young men from the community. Olive was seeing a man named Roy Crawford, and Nell was in a relationship with Jim Wilcox, the son of the local sheriff. By November 1901, Jim and Nell had been seeing each other for two years, and things were serious enough that the subject of marriage was becoming a regular topic of conversation.

On the evening of November 20, both Roy and Jim went to the Cropsey home, as they had many evenings before. The two couples spent the evening together, and around 11:00 p.m., Jim stood up and asked Nell if she would go with him to the front porch to talk in private. Olive and Roy remained inside until Roy left about fifteen minutes later. By then, everyone else in the house had fallen asleep. After about half an hour, there was no one on the front porch. Olive assumed that Nell had come back into the house and gone to bed or had come back in the house without being heard and was in one of the private sitting rooms with Jim. So, Olive went to bed.

All seemed well until a little after midnight, when the Cropseys' dog started barking and wouldn't stop. As the dog's barks got louder, the family woke up and made their way to the front yard. The evening was cool, and the family soon realized that Nell was not in the front yard with them, so they returned to the house to see why she had not been awakened by the dog's frenzied barking. After checking her bed and finding it had not been slept in, they frantically searched the house, only to find their worst nightmare: Nell was missing.

Another search of the house confirmed the family's worst fears, and Mary Cropsey began to panic. In an effort to bring her some peace of mind, her husband said that with all the talk of marriage, the young couple may very well have left in the night to elope. Nell had been excited about a possible upcoming trip to New York, so maybe the couple had gone together. At least, under the circumstances, that's what they hoped had happened. But no one really believed that was what had happened. Nell's clothes were still in her room. The luggage she would have taken with her was still in its place, and there was no sign she had ever gone back in the house.

That being the case, William Cropsey went to the home of Sherriff W.T. Wilcox to see if Jim was there. And that's where the case took an odd turn. When the men asked Jim to come into the parlor to talk to Nell's father, he refused. As William Cropsey asked the young man to talk to him and tell him what happened, Jim continued to refuse. William Cropsey was desperate, because Jim had been the last person to see Nell alive. The panicked father saw him as his last resort to find out where his daughter might be. Still, Jim refused to talk to the distraught father.

In a last-ditch effort to make the young man talk and give the family some indication of what happened that night, William Cropsey went to see Chief of Police W.C. Dawson. After their meeting, the police forced Jim to return to William and Mary's home, where he was interrogated for hours. Regardless of what he was asked or how much pressure the law enforcement representatives and the distraught parents put on him, Jim's story (devoid of any actual helpful information) did not change. He reiterated several times that he had asked Nell to accompany him to the porch as he was leaving, they had a ten-minute conversation and, when he left, she was in tears. He gave no reason for why she was upset.

The one positive outcome of the night was that the police were able to rule out suicide. Nell was so looking forward to the New York trip and was in such a good mood because of it, there was no reason to believe she was suicidal. But Jim refused to provide any information about why she was so upset when he left. Another interesting fact the police found was that Nell had been having trouble with her right foot. That being the case, it was unlikely that she had been able to run away and was likely carried off the front porch.

Soon, news of the disappearance of Nell Cropsey from her riverside home was not just common knowledge but was becoming a national sensation. Bloodhounds, detectives, divers and even a psychic were brought in to search for her. Amid the increased activity, word of Jim's temper came to light and began to spread. According to statements made during the investigation, Olive said Nell and Jim had met about two months after the family moved to Elizabeth City. At first, James came to see Nell every Sunday. Later, he went to their house almost every afternoon. Jim and Nell would go on walks and rides, and they would sail and see shows. But in the fall of 1901, things took a darker turn, and the couple started getting into arguments. Nell's family and other people recalled witnessing heated arguments between the two, and some began to speculate that Nell, instead of looking forward to marrying her suitor, was, in fact, making plans to break off their relationship. But if that was the case, she never had the chance. On December 27, 1901, the unthinkable happened.

Nell's body was discovered. Her corpse was found floating down the Pasquotank River, and all speculation about her eloping or leaving for New York early was silenced. Since the river had been searched previously, the police determined that Nell's murderer had recently retrieved her body from wherever it had been originally and dumped it in the river. Amid death threats and the threat of a public lynching, Jim was arrested and put in jail. The three main factors that made his case almost cut and dry were Jim's temper, the fact that he could not account for his whereabouts after he left the Cropsey house on November 20 and the autopsy report. Nell had received a massive blow to her left temple.

As things progressed in the case against Jim Wilcox, he waived his right to a preliminary hearing. In March 1902, he was found guilty of first-degree murder and was sentenced to be hanged. Before he reached the gallows, his case was declared a mistrial by the North Carolina Supreme Court. He was retried in 1903, and this time, he was found guilty of second-degree murder. Jim was sentenced to thirty years in jail.

According to the March 13, 1941 issue of the *Daily Advance* (the newspaper of record for the case), Jim's father tried several times to have Jim pardoned through petitions. The pardons were denied by governors on two separate occasions, most likely because of Jim's attitude during the search for Nell and toward the Cropsey family during the trial. In 1918, however, Jim was pardoned by Governor Thomas Bickett after he wrote to the governor and declared his innocence. This time, Jim was more contrite and admitted he was uncooperative when the murder first occurred.

In 1918, with half his sentence served, Jim was released from prison. A few years later, Jim met with W.O. Saunders, and the two agreed to collaborate on a book about the Cropsey murder case. Saunders was a prominent newspaper editor, politician and spokesman on state and national affairs and was more than qualified to take on such a project. But here, Nell's story takes another macabre turn. Not long after their meeting, Jim died by suicide via a shotgun blast to the head. And not long after Jim's death, Saunders, while on his way from Elizabeth City to Norfolk, drowned after his car plunged off the highway and into a Great Dismal Swamp Canal. So, whatever Jim told the famed editor went with both men to their graves.

But the story does not stop there. The spirit of the vivacious and beautiful Nell continues to make its presence known to this day. The reports of Nell remaining active in her riverside home are numerous. Lights are turned on and off, doors open and shut, water rushes from the sink—even when no one turns the handle—and strange cold gusts of air waft through the house without explanation. There are also stories from people who claim they have seen a pale young woman walking through empty rooms. Even people passing by on the street have seen the same pale figure looking out at them from an upstairs window. Maybe she is hoping that, one day, justice will be served for her untimely death.

4

DEATH DREAM

Is it possible to predict your own death?
Fannie Pearl MacWilliams could tell you.

Some things are hard, if not impossible, to explain. Take the story of Fannie Pearl MacWilliams Wahab for example. Born in September 1894 to John and Elizabeth MacWilliams, she grew up within sight of the Ocracoke Lighthouse. That fact is not so much an important part of the story itself, but the lighthouse is an important landmark that helps put the area during that time into perspective. Back in the 1800s, Ocracoke Island was unofficially divided into the "creek side," which included the north side of the harbor, and the "point side" of the island, which comprised the area around the lighthouse and the additional area to south. Fannie Pearl MacWilliams was raised on the point side of the island. Her father, John MacWilliams, owned a collection of retail stores and a dock on the water referred to as the Department Store. The equivalent of today's shopping center, the Department Store was one of the main retail establishments in Ocracoke.

Prior to 1939, what is now the harbor was called "the creek" (or Cockle Creek), and it connected to the Pamlico Sound via a small inlet most locals called "the ditch." During Fannie Pearl MacWilliams Wahab's time, there was a definite distinction between the people who lived "'round creek" (also known as creekers) and the people who lived "down point" (also known as pointers). The rivalry between the two factions was good-natured, and people new to the island soon became part of the community as either "creekers" or "pointers." The division was further emphasized on the east side by the creek, which extended through Ocracoke Village and essentially divided it into two distinct parts.

Eventually, a series of footbridges were built along the creek, but due to their size, horses and carts could not cross them. So more often than not, people had to walk on the paths on either side of the creek. And if they had items to carry, they used some kind of small handcart, wheelbarrow or other method to carry goods from one place to another, regardless of the distance. And foot travel could be difficult on the sandy trails along the creek if the person was managing a large load. But despite distances, creeks, moderately passable bridges and the fact that life on the island had its inconveniences, its people were self-sufficient, and the area still had some of the same advantages of the mainland.

One of the island's advantages was a school located in the Odd Fellow's lodge. The building was originally built as a lodge for the Independent Order of Odd Fellows. But the building served double duty, with Ocracoke's K-12 school operating on the first floor until a new school was built in 1917. This lodge/school was where Fannie Pearl MacWilliams and most of the other children on the island attended school. One of the teachers there was Robert Stanley Wahab, a native of Ocracoke. Stanley grew up on the island and in 1904 went to sea on the menhaden schooner *Fanny Sprague* and then served as a seaman on *Dredge No. Three* of the Norfolk Dredging Company. Later, during his time as a crewman on a luxury yacht owned by industrialist T. Coleman du Pont, his life changed. Coleman du Pont suggested that Stanley go to school, and after some urging, he agreed and attended the Goldey Business College in Delaware. Next, because of his newly acquired education, Stanley Wahab held a number of jobs in businesses specializing in provisions. In 1910, he returned to Ocracoke as a teacher with a background in business.

And as it sometimes happens, the teacher and his student, Fannie Pearl MacWilliams, fell in love. Even Fannie Pearl's subsequent move to Marshallberg, North Carolina, to finish school did not quench the flame between the two lovers. They continued to see each other, despite the fact that the trip from the island to Marshallberg was a little over fifty miles (ferry ride included), quite a trip back in those days. But their love continued to grow, and they would not be dissuaded. And in 1911, the two were married.

Not long after their wedding, Stanley accepted a teaching position in Norfolk, Virginia. And soon after the move, seventeen-year-old Fannie Pearl MacWilliams Wahab discovered she was pregnant. In those days, it was not uncommon for women to stay with their family until their baby was born, so Fannie Pearl went back to Ocracoke Island and stayed with her husband's mother, Martha Ann Howard Wahab. Martha Ann lived "'round creek" on the island. Stanley stayed in Richmond so he could continue working, though he supported his wife in every way, including sending her money, to enable her to be surrounded by loved ones and wait for the birth of their first child. And as the old saying goes, everything was fine until it wasn't.

One morning, Fannie Pearl woke up with an overwhelming sense of deep sorrow. She tried all morning to free herself of the feeling. She tried to find a way to move forward, but the melancholy was too strong. Finally, she confided to Martha Ann that the previous night, she'd had a horrible dream and was still feeling the effects of it. In the dream, she watched herself die. Then, to add to her horror, she saw herself dressed in white, lying in a white casket and moving silently along the water in a white sailboat.

The water sparkled a muted silver, and as the clouds moved and shifted in front of the full moon, the sailboat was alternately bathed in moonlight and an eerie silver glow. The sailboat continued its unearthly voyage along the silent, glittering waterway. Fannie Pearl's terror increased with each passing moment until she awoke in a sweat. And though she was awake, the image of the sailboat of death remained vivid in her mind. All day long, she was plagued by images of her body in the coffin, the full moon, her journey into the unknown.

And the next night, Fannie Pearl MacWilliams Wahab died, as did the child she carried. As soon as her death and the death of her child were confirmed, steps were taken to contact Stanley Wahab and break the tragic news to him. With no phone on the island, a message was relayed to Stanley by the coast guard via a ship-to-shore phone call. The news was devastating, but in his grief, Stanley told the family he would make the initial preparations and to do nothing until he arrived on the island. Then he set about making his wife's final arrangements and finding some way to get home as soon as possible.

Stanley bought a beautiful casket, wanting something fine enough to honor the woman he loved. Then he made arrangements to ride on the mail boat when it arrived the next day. Though he had made arrangements as fast as he could, it was still late in the day when the mail boat arrived. Once the casket was loaded and Stanley was on board, the boat left the dock, and Stanley and his precious cargo began their somber trip to Ocracoke Island.

Things progressed quickly once Stanley returned to the island. In those days, bodies were buried as soon as possible, since there was no way to

A simple white casket. To some, it is a hand-crafted thing of beauty. To Fannie Pearl MacWilliams Wahab, it was the stuff of nightmares. © Antonio *Oquias*.

embalm a body on the island. There were no such facilities on Ocracoke. And since Fannie Pearl had been dead more than twenty-four hours, it was imperative that she be buried without delay. In fact, the rest of the preparations moved at such a fast pace that once Stanley arrived on Ocracoke, there was no opportunity for Martha Ann to tell her son about Fannie Pearl's nightmare. So, there was nothing she could do but keep quiet and watch as they put Fannie Pearl MacWilliams Wahab's body in the beautiful solid white casket her husband had purchased.

With Fannie Pearl's body ready for burial, there was still the question of the best way to bring her body to the cemetery. Because even though she had died "down creek," the family's burial place was "down point." And the trek to her burial spot, which was on a part of the island near her father's store and dock complex, would require carrying the coffin from her in-laws' home, down long, sandy lanes and across planks and footbridges that crossed the smaller creeks (called "guts"), all the way to the other side of the harbor.

Instead of asking people to carry the coffin by hand across such challenging terrain, Stanley placed the white casket on a white skiff and started across the creek, trailed by family, friends and other members of the funeral procession in rowboats. And there beneath the night sky, illuminated by a full moon, Fannie Pearl MacWilliams Wahab was carried to her final resting place, dressed in white and in a white casket on board a white sailing skiff, exactly the way it happened in her dream.

Macabre note: This story has a morbid little postscript. Normally, the last line in this story would be the end. But here's a little something to bring the scary part of the story home and sort of tie everything up in a neat little bow of black funeral crepe. Because of dark tourism and some people's over-fascination with true stories of the supernatural, Fannie Pearl's grave is marked with a "No Trespassing" sign in an effort to dissuade people from trying to recreate their own paranormal experience at her final resting place. Maybe that will help her rest in peace.

5

THE BURGWIN-WRIGHT HOUSE

*Despite being built on the site of a jail known for its appalling conditions
and standing witness to slavery and other powerful events,
what caused the house to finally "wake up"?*

Wilmington, North Carolina, is home to many fascinating historic buildings. The Bellamy Mansion, the Burgwin-Wright House, the Dudley Mansion, the Honnet House and the Latimer House are just a few. Each one is a showplace, the best of the best, a tribute to the architect's vision and the builder's skill. But in addition to being superb examples of the architecture of their respective eras, many of the historic buildings in Wilmington have something else in common: they're haunted.

Take the Burgwin-Wright House, for example. With its large front door with two windows on each side, coupled with its grand columns (all of which are mirrored along the back of the house), the house is an impressive example of the Georgian style of architecture. In fact, it is the only house from the colonial period in Wilmington that is still open to the public. The house was built in 1770 for John Burgwin and his wife on the site of an old jail, the ballast stones of which were used in building the home's foundation. The house has a colorful and exciting history, and John Burgwin's history is almost as colorful as that of the house.

John served as quartermaster for the New Hanover County militia in 1754. Between 1756 and 1759, he served as clerk of the Bladen County Court. In addition, he was an attorney commissioned before the Cumberland County

Court from 1758 to 1761. He was appointed clerk of the Superior Court of Justices for the District of Wilmington in 1768 and was appointed treasurer of the Province of North Carolina in 1767. Governor Tryon appointed him register of the Court of Chancery in May 1769, and the next day, he appointed him master of the High Court of Chancery. John also served as Wilmington's town commissioner from 1769 to 1775 and as a member of the general assembly in Bladen County in 1773. Although this was an active and productive time for John, it was also marred by tragedy. John's wife, Margaret, died before their home was completed.

In 1782, while John was living in England, he married Elizabeth Bush, also known as Eliza. In 1784, they moved to America and lived in the Hermitage in Castle Hayne (another property built for John Burgwin). John rented the original house on the corner of Third and Market Streets in Wilmington to Charles Jewkes, a former business partner. Charles brought with him his wife, Ann Grainger Wright, and her three children from her first marriage. The Jewkes family remained there through the end of the Revolutionary War, even living in the house during the time General Cornwallis used it as his headquarters.

There are still outdoor and sub-basement jail cells and a freestanding cookhouse with a massive hearth on the property. So, considering the house's wide-ranging history and the site on which it was built, it only stands to reason that the Burgwin-White House would be the site of paranormal activity, although the house had been "quiet" for decades. In 1937, the property was purchased by the National Society of the Colonial Dames of America. In 1939, restoration efforts began on the outside of the house, and the project was completed in 1941. And at some point, the house "woke up." It seems the first manifestations began around seventy years ago during one of the first Azalea Festival Tours. That afternoon, members of one tour group got more than they bargained for.

At the height of the tour, a museum docent's attention was drawn to the antique spinning wheel that sits in the corner of one of the rooms. The wheel, which had been stuck for years, began to turn. At first, it moved slowly. And then, with increased vigor, the wheel began making a constant *clack…clack…clack…clack*. Faster and faster, it turned, the whirring and clicking of the wheel creating a steady hum. Then it stopped just as abruptly as it had started. Some of the braver members of the tour group, once the shock had worn off, made their way over to the spinning wheel and attempted to turn it. It wouldn't budge. The wheel was frozen in place, stuck fast, just as it had been for years.

Some people report hearing voices in the slave quarters. © *Publicdomainphotos, Dreamstime.com.*

But the wheel is only the beginning. Witnesses have seen apparitions walking in the hallways—men in knee britches and women in more formal Edwardian dress; women in hats and long-sleeved dresses and men in suits, overcoats and bowlers/top hats. Paranormal investigators who have come to study the house are not told anything about what other investigators have found, but once a new investigation is complete, it corroborates the paranormal findings of previous investigations. The specter in the hall has even been caught on camera twice.

While making preparations to take a group of children on a tour, one of the educators associated with the house heard footsteps on the floor above her. She looked up and saw a man in period clothing walking in front of a door at the top of the stairs. Thinking it was the other educator who was to assist her on the tour, she waited for him to come downstairs. While she waited, she noted the man's clothes were a different color than those normally worn during the reenactments, but she didn't think much about it—not until the employee's entrance door opened near her. The educator she was expecting walked in wearing completely different clothes from those she had seen just minutes before.

One of the museum's regular docents would always close the door to the Blue Room at the end of the day, only to find it open the next morning.

And other reliable witnesses have heard voices, sobbing, muffled coughs and bits of quiet conversation coming from unoccupied rooms in the house. And on more than one occasion, witnesses have caught a glimpse of something or someone walking past their doorway in an otherwise unoccupied hallway.

6

THE ATTMORE-OLIVER HOUSE

Miss Mary is not someone to be trifled with, even after death.

The Attmore-Oliver House in New Bern has an interesting history. It was originally built in 1790 for Samuel Chapman, a retired officer in the Continental Army. Chapman was a second lieutenant at the start of the Revolutionary War and was later promoted to first lieutenant and eventually captain. He served with that rank through the end of the war. Upon returning home, he became the clerk of the Craven County Supreme Court. When he died in 1807, his daughter, Caroline, inherited the house.

Caroline lived in the house for twenty-seven years. Then in 1834, Caroline sold the house to Isaac Taylor and moved to New York. Taylor was a successful merchant in town, and he bought the story-and-a-half house for his daughter Mary and her husband, George Sitgreaves Attmore. The only problem was, their family was growing, so they needed more space than the house offered in its current state. So, the house was enlarged and remodeled, using elements of the Greek-Revival style that was popular at the time.

Eventually, the house went to the Attmores' oldest daughter, Hannah Taylor Attmore, and her husband, William Hollister Oliver. Their daughter, Mary Taylor Oliver, inherited the house in 1908 and was the last person to live there. When she died, her nephews inherited the house. Instead of living in the house, they sold it to the New Bern Historical Society. "Miss Mary," as she was known, was something of a colorful character during her lifetime, and remains so even after her death. Poltergeist activity in the house has been attributed to the people who died of smallpox in the house and to Miss

Mary herself. A manifestation that has come to be known as the Kit-Kat-Stomp is one example, but more on that later.

Miss Mary was set in her ways and wanted things done a certain way. More than once, she arrived at church to find someone sitting in "her place" on a certain pew and asked them to move. She was what people today would refer to as a force of nature. But her forceful attitude wasn't reserved for ordering her daily life. She also did not like animals—cats in particular. As the story is told, Miss Mary had a problem with cats coming into her yard. She hired a local man to "dispose of" the cats. When the job was completed, the man went to Miss Mary for his pay, and she refused to pay him. When it became obvious that she had no intention of paying what she promised, the man left—but not before he had the final say.

Later that day, Miss Mary looked out of an upstairs window and saw the man had reburied the cats with their heads sticking up above the ground. Miss Mary became incensed and allegedly stomped around her room for days in frustration. Today, visitors and employees alike report hearing a noise that sounds like someone stomping their feet upstairs, hence the name Kit-Kat-Stomp. But Miss Mary's activity is not the only manifestation that has been noticed in the house. Many people have watched as a cabinet door opens by itself, only to close again a few minutes later.

Sometimes, people downstairs will hear someone moving around in the otherwise empty upstairs area. Other times, people will hear someone they assume to be Miss Mary rummaging around in her bedroom. But Miss Mary is not the only source of paranormal activity. During the renovation, medical supplies and other artifacts were discovered, leading to the supposition that the house served as a hospital during the Civil War. Some family members did serve as soldiers and fought for the Confederacy, so it is quite possible that those soldiers—and some patients who died from smallpox—also remain in the house. In 2006, the North Carolina Ghost Hunters Society conducted a formal investigation of the house. The group discovered energy fields and took photographs that captured glowing orbs. The resulting report indicated that there is definitely a presence that can't be explained in the house.

7

THE THALIAN HALL SPECTERS

The show must go on, and for some dedicated thespians, it goes on after death.

In *Brushstrokes of a Gadfly*, E.A. Bucchianeri wrote, "Theatres are curious places, magician's trick-boxes where the golden memories of dramatic triumphs linger like nostalgic ghosts, and where the unexplainable, the fantastic, the tragic, the comic and the absurd are routine occurrences on and off the stage." Some actors and cast members from the past are not quite "living" proof of this sentiment. But even death can't keep them from enjoying a production or two in one of North Carolina's most historic theaters.

Thalian Hall had a humble beginning. Thanks in part to a bequest from Colonel James Innis, the trustees of the Wilmington Academy started raising funds in 1803 to build a new theater facility. The resulting building was seventy feet long by forty feet wide and thirty feet high, including the foundation, and was called Innes Academy. A local group of actors called the Thalian Theater Group began performing there on a regular basis to the enthusiastic encouragement of the community. And as word of the theater and community support spread, major touring companies put the Innes Academy on their schedule and performed between productions of the Thalian Theater Group. As the venue flourished, there was a growing feeling that the facility should expand. And while the exact catalyst for this is subject to debate, one popular story includes a famous singer's refusal to perform in the facility.

As the story is told, Jenny Lind, a world-renowned singer known as the "Swedish Nightingale," was on her way to Charleston to perform. Some of the more prominent people in town knew of her plans, and when her train made a stop in Wilmington, they met it with much fanfare. They showered her with praise, presented her with dozens of flowers and then made their request. They asked if she would consider singing at Innes Academy while she was in town. Miss Lind's manager asked about the size of the venue. When he heard the dimensions, he said, "Gentlemen, my orchestra would fill a large part of that space."

Since the facility could not accommodate her show, she continued her journey and performed in Charleston, leaving the townspeople of Wilmington to bemoan the fact that they had lost out on a world-class performer. The leading citizens of Wilmington decided they would never be put in such an embarrassing position again. They reasoned that, as the largest city in the state with a port and a rail center that made travel to places as far away as New York and even Europe possible, Wilmington needed a larger performance facility. With that motivation, plans were developed, and construction began. And in 1858, with much of the scaffolding still in place, Thalian Hall hosted its first performance. Because of the popularity of the entertainment provided at the new facility, soon, there was a performance in the building every night.

The hall presented amateur productions, stock performances, minstrel shows, operas, musical comedies, dances, a show featuring a tightrope walker and shows that featured animals, including sled dogs, three live bears, two St. Bernard dogs and a circus play with three ponies, a trained donkey and a horse. There was literally something for everyone. But as times changed, so did people's interests. Presentations changed from concerts and plays to panoramas, or massive canvas paintings, some as large as 1,800 feet wound on large spools, depicting places and events. People were transported to grand destinations without leaving the theater. But entertainment was not the only purpose for which the theater was used. With the rapidly changing political climate of the day, the hall was used for political rallies and meetings, many of which focused on the coming Civil War.

During the war, the hall was leased to private individuals and theater companies. It hosted road shows as well as more widely known attractions and performers from 1860 to 1936. In fact, from 1867 to 1871, John T. Ford, the promoter who had owned Ford's Theatre (where Lincoln was shot), leased Thalian Hall and changed its name to the Wilmington Opera House. The last of the nation's great road shows, the *Ziegfeld Follies*, was performed there in 1929, but by this time, the building was in need of renovation, and various projects to save the building were undertaken through 1940. After World War II, a new set of renovations was undertaken, followed by more renovations in the 1970s after a small fire started in the downstairs part of the hall. In 1975, when the building had been restored to its former glory, there was a resurgence of concerts, shows and other performances, the result of which was a massive increase in attendance. To keep up with the expanding schedule of performances, both professional and local, the theater required more renovation and expansion projects, which were undertaken through the 1990s.

And somewhere in all of the renovation and change, something happened. In the process designed to improve and expand the historic theater, something woke up. Two men and one woman, actors in their "former" life, have been seen on many occasions. The three spectral thespians, dressed in Edwardian clothing, have been seen watching plays on many occasions. They will sometimes linger in the balcony during rehearsals. But there is also evidence that they do more than watch. Actors, stagehands and others involved in various productions have experienced cold spots and felt a strong presence in the lobby, the changing rooms, the corridor and even the bathrooms. There have been cases of people hearing voices coming from empty corridors and rooms, and the specters have even been known to move tools, scripts, makeup and other items.

But not all those who haunt the venerable facility are so easily recognizable. For example, there's an inexplicable story about a director's dog. As the story is told, the dog wandered up into the balcony during a rehearsal. Suddenly, an unseen something grabbed the dog and hurled it over the balcony, where it fell two floors to the ground. But instead of crashing to the floor, something else—something unseen, but no less real—caught the little dog and saved it from a gruesome end.

So, what caused the building to "wake up"? Some who study paranormal events say that building renovations can trigger such activity in a formerly dormant building. However, in the case of Thalian Hall, there could be another contributing factor. What no one knew for many years was that the building had been constructed on a Native burial ground. In 1983, an arm and jawbone were found during the renovation that had begun the same year, and more bones were discovered in 2009. The bones were most likely there before the building was built in 1803. Their owners have been patiently resting but, evidently, not in peace.

8

THE BELLAMY MANSION

*A history of sickness and fire and the specter of war
seem to have triggered something in the house.*

In 1860, Wilmington was the largest city in North Carolina, a major cosmopolitan port city. It was the kind of place where a man like Dr. John Bellamy could thrive both professionally and culturally. And to that end, one of his first acts there was to construct a magnificent home using the labor of enslaved and free artisans. Dr. Bellamy hired Wilmington architect James F. Post, who had supervised the construction of Thalian Hall in Wilmington, to oversee the construction of the twenty-two-room mansion. Like many of the stately homes in Wilmington, the Bellamy Mansion is a marvelous example of the antebellum architecture that was so popular during the 1850s and 1860s. With its mixture of Neoclassical architectural styles (including Greek Revival and Italianate) and grand wrap-around porches, the mansion was a showplace in every sense of the word.

When the Bellamys were prepared to move into their mansion on Market Street, their family included eight children aged one to nineteen years. And Dr. Bellamy's wife, Eliza, was pregnant with their tenth child. Over the years, the Bellamy Mansion was home to two generations of Bellamy family members. And tragically, half a dozen family members died in the house.

But far from being just another large home in a prominent city, the Bellamy Mansion has an interesting past. For example, the home was taken over by federal troops during the Civil War. In January 1865, Fort Fisher fell to the Northern forces, and since it was the last source of protection for the port city, it was just a matter of time before the Union forces headed into Wilmington. Dr. Bellamy, who was then currently residing with his family at Grovely Plantation following a yellow fever outbreak in Wilmington, knew he and his family could not return home. On February 22, Union officers took shelter in the city's nicer homes whose owners had been forced to abandon them. The Bellamy House was quickly occupied and converted into headquarters for military staff.

In April 1865, at the end of the Civil War, the federal government seized the mansion and its surrounding property and denied Dr. Bellamy access to his home. In addition to being a doctor, Bellamy was a plantation owner and businessman. Because of the large number of people he had enslaved prior to the war, the doctor had to go through a lengthy process to reclaim his physical property. In the summer of 1865, he received a presidential pardon from President Andrew Johnson, which allowed him to reclaim his plantation land and commercial buildings—but not the house on Market Street. It took three additional years for Dr. Bellamy to reclaim his home. But that was not the end of the mansion's troubled history.

As late as February 1972, the fourth generation of Bellamy family members who lived in Wilmington started Bellamy Mansion Inc. in an effort to preserve and restore the magnificent home. But one month after the establishment of the foundation, arsonists set fire to the mansion. The fire department was able to put out the fire but not before the home's interior sustained extensive damage. And while the story has a happy ending and the mansion is now a fully functioning museum of history and design arts, the mansion is not without its secrets and strange occurrences.

For example, guests in the mansion sometimes feel drawn to the third floor. Since the third floor is known as the Children's Floor, you would expect it to be a happy place. And during the Bellamys' time in the home, it was. But in recent years, visitors to the Children's Floor have reported having a sense of dread or unease when they arrived in that section of the house. Some have even felt sick. Then there is the case of Ellen Douglas Bellamy. Ellen lived in the mansion until her death. In her later years, she enjoyed reading the newspaper every night before she went to sleep. Her fingers would become smudged with printer's ink, so when she went to extinguish the candle in the sconce, she left black smudges on the wall. That in itself is not unusual at all. However, the smudges still reappear, even after the room has been repainted many times.

What exactly chased a film crew out of the house during a movie shoot? © *Marie-claire Lander.*

Perhaps the most striking event happened in 1990 while a film crew was working in the mansion. They were in the library, and as one crew member related the incident, "We had locked the door behind us and were completely alone in the house when suddenly, we heard the heavy front door open and slam shut with a loud bang. A cold blast of air rushed through the closed door up the stairs and into the library....Our papers sailed in every direction. Within seconds, we were out of there....We heard the library door slam shut...followed by an angry pounding on the door."

Did the film crew have an honest to goodness brush with the supernatural? Did something not want them in the house? Was it just a series of natural phenomena coupled with bad timing on the part of the film crew? Or is the answer more paranormal than normal?

9

THE TOWN OF MURFREESBORO

It's one thing to have haunted sites in a town.
It's quite another when the entire town seems to be haunted.

While Murfreesboro is more a part of the "Inner Banks" of North Carolina, both its proximity to the coast and its abundance of paranormal events make it a welcome addition to our tour of the haunted North Carolina Coast. And in the case of Murfreesboro, there is not just a single landmark that seems to be haunted. No, in this case, the whole town seems to be a haven for supernatural activity. There are very few places you can go in Murfreesboro where there is not a haunted site or a place that harbors eerie tales of strange occurrences.

Well before the land was settled in the 1700s, what is now known as Murfreesboro was inhabited by the Meherrin, Chowanoke and Nottaway Native tribes. And while there had been land transactions in the early 1700s, William Hardee Murfree, an Irish immigrant, purchased a large tract of land in 1746, which became Murfree's Landing. Shortly after it was established, the site became a King's Landing, where representatives of the king had the right to inspect all goods coming in and going out of the port by ship.

As the port prospered, so did the surrounding area. Now known as Murfreesboro, agriculture and educational facilities became the hallmark of the region. But all was not well. As often happens in history, the growth was beset by illness and tragedy. Tuberculosis, the Spanish flu and polio took their toll on the town through the years, as did the Revolutionary War, the Civil War and other tragedies. Still, the town adapted and ultimately thrived. Still, even as things returned to normal, the town became a haven for the paranormal. Don't believe me? Come on. We'll take a short tour around town.

COLLEGE LIFE AND AFTERLIFE

Chowan University (One University Place)

Chowan University began its existence as Chowan Baptist Female Institute. The four-year women's college was founded by Godwin Cotton Moore in 1848, and administrative offices were constructed in 1851. By 1867, the name of the school was changed to Chowan Female Collegiate Institute and then changed back to the original name, Chowan Baptist Female Institute. The school kept the name until 1910. At that point, the school was expanding its academic offerings and was awarding baccalaureate degrees. Twenty-one years later, the college admitted its first male students.

By 1937, due, in great part, to the effects of the Great Depression, Chowan College was forced to become a two-year institution. This status lasted until 1992. By this point, the college had developed a junior class and returned to operating as a four-year institution. Things continued to progress, and in 2006, the former college became Chowan University. It continues to thrive and provide a quality education in over seventy academic disciplines, and it has a solid athletic program. And from that solid preparation for life come professional athletes, business leaders and politicians.

But probably the most famous former student attended the school in 1886. And she still visits the campus every year in October—on Halloween. She is dressed in the same brown taffeta that she favored when she lived on campus. Her name is Eolene Davidson. But she is better known at Chowan University and around the town of Murfreesboro as the "Brown Lady." Oddly enough, history had almost forgotten her name. And the cause of her death is still uncertain. But her story is brought back into sharp focus every October 31 when she makes her return to campus.

Eolene attended the fledgling college when it was in its thirty-eighth year. Back then, it was called the Chowan Baptist Female Institute; this was after it was renamed and then its original name was restored. Eolene resided in the Columns Building and was known for wearing brown taffeta everywhere.

The rustling of her skirts was a common sound, and her choice of dress was the main reason she later became known as the Brown Lady. Oddly enough, even her name has sometimes come into question.

In 1915, student Jessie Maie Piland wrote, "Among the many fair-haired and energetic girls that were preparing for college this beautiful September was Eolene Davidson, the beautiful daughter of a well-known farmer. She was a pleasant, sweet-natured girl of nineteen, tall and slender, with wavy black hair, fair complexion and dreamy blue eyes. Much did she enjoy the pleasures of life."

Still, some others who recount her tragic life say little more than, "Her name is lost to history." But while her identity is not in question for our purposes, how she died is. The most cited account says that early in her scholastic career, she went to visit a friend in New York City, and while she was there, she met a young attorney named James Lorrene. The two fell in love, and before she made the journey back to college, James proposed. She agreed but said she wanted to finish her education first. So, she went back to the college and resumed her studies. However, Eolene contracted typhoid fever in early October her sophomore year. As she lay dying in her bed, her fiancé, James, was informed of her condition. Her young suitor made the trip to Murfreesboro from New York as fast as was possible in those days. Sadly, though, he arrived on November 1—too late. Eolene had died the night before, on Halloween.

Is that what happened? In another version of the story, Eolene met and fell in love with a handsome young soldier while in college. The two were serious and made plans to marry. But her young soldier still had to fulfill his duty, and he went where he was sent, as good soldiers do. So, Eolene went about her days studying and spending time with her friends. And more often than not, she was dressed in her usual brown taffeta, skirt swishing and rustling in her wake in what was becoming her "trademark" of sorts. And all was well until the news came to her that her fiancé had been killed. Eolene was devastated by the news and immediately took to her bed. She died the very same night. Some say she died from a broken heart. A few other accounts imply that Eolene jumped to her death from the roof of her dormitory, her handkerchief fluttering after.

But regardless of the cause of her death, it is always said to have happened on Halloween. And to this day, the Brown Lady makes her presence known by turning lights on and off and opening and closing doors. And if you listen carefully, you will most likely hear her footsteps—and possibly the swish and rustle of brown taffeta—on the third floor of the Columns Building, all on

The pathways on Chowan University lead to centers of education—and the supernatural. © *The Ghost Guild*.

the anniversary of her death, Halloween. But don't be lulled into thinking she is the only spectral entity at the university. Oh, no.

The university has a few more ghostly tenants on its roster. Take Belk Hall for example. It's a nice, quiet, three-story residence hall that was renovated in 2015. It's the kind of place that feels like a home away from home to the 210 female freshman students who live there. But even with the public safety facility nearby, something is going on in the residence hall. The young women are never completely alone. It is said that, years ago, a little girl rode her tricycle down the stairs and was killed. And to this day, students and visitors alike say you can still hear the voice of a little girl laughing. Then the laughs turn to screams on the stairs.

In another room in the same residence hall, a student died by suicide many years ago. Even today, people report a definite eerie presence in the room at times. It is rumored that previous occupants of the room have even gone crazy there. Travel about three-quarters of the way down the campus, and you will come to Mixon Hall. That's the residence hall for upperclassmen. It's situated near Garrison Stadium, the university's first-rate football stadium. Sometimes, people will see the spectral shape of a young man roaming the second floor of Mixon Hall. He's said to be same young man who hanged himself from the staircase in the residence hall so many years ago. And the final undead resident "lives" in Daniel Hall, the music hall. This specter can most often be found playing the piano in one of the rooms. But it's best to listen from outside, because if you enter the room, there will be no one at the piano.

A DOCTOR BY ANY OTHER NAME...

The Conjure Doctor (409 Williams Street)

James "Jim" Jordan (pronounced Jer-dan) was known as the Conjure Doctor to the people in Murfreesboro and, eventually, around the world. Born to formerly enslaved parents in 1871, Jim got much of his knowledge of folk healing from his family. His father, Isaac, was a sharecropper and lay preacher. His mother, Harriet, was a homemaker and weaver. She was the person who introduced her son to folk medical traditions. A conjurer uncle taught him herbal medicine and the art of divination, or fortune telling, with a deck of cards in the early 1890s.

Early on, his family sharecropped on the farm of inventor Henry Gatling. Gatling took a special interest in Jim and used to read his "little black book of magic" to the young boy. The book was most likely about nineteenth-century Hermetic, or European-based, magic. When Jim was eight years old, Gatling was murdered, but the inventor had already had a profound effect on the young boy. Jordan said on more than one occasion of Henry Gatling, "No better man ever lived."

Between Gatling and Jim's relatives who were practitioners on some level of root work or hoodoo, Jim Jordan's studies branched out into psychology, systems of divination, herbal medicine, palmistry and spiritual counseling. While working as a farmer and a logger, Jordan became the apprentice of Old Edloe, a local conjure doctor. He studied with Old Edloe until his death in 1900. But it wasn't until 1927 that Jordan left his farming and logging jobs to become a full-time conjure doctor. And by this time, the fifty-year-old Jordan had something of a reputation as one of the best conjure doctors around. As a conjure doctor he would be asked by those who came to him to do many things, including establishing good or bad luck, telling the future, retrieving lost items, inducing sickness or death or healing those afflicted with ailments.

He often used a crystal ball that he said was created when lightning struck a cypress tree. Legend has it that the crystal ball was once stolen by a visitor. As the thief attempted to make his getaway, his car caught on fire and could only be extinguished when the crystal ball was returned to Jordan. People believed that Jordan could communicate with spirits and see the future in his crystal ball. It is even said that he was able to use the crystal ball to locate the body of a missing boy near Winton, North Carolina, when the authorities were unable to do so. But not all of his work was deemed helpful. His work with uncrossings (working to deliver someone from negative psychic energy, hexes or curses) led many to believe he was a practitioner of black magic.

Even so, locals respected him, partly out of fear of potential magic reprisals. And even so, many medical doctors said it was not unusual for Jordan to refer patients to them when he felt he could not help them. In addition to his conjure doctor business, Jordan also went into other lines of business, including running a country store, more farming and logging and mule and horse trading. Jordan was so successful (bringing in the equivalent of $10,000 per year), he invested in a sandlot baseball team called the Como Eagles. He had so many enterprises during his first fifteen years in business that the hundreds of people (including family) he employed became known as Jordanville.

HENRY GATLING'S GHOST (437 WILLIAMS STREET)

The Gatling family cemetery is all that remains of the homestead that produced two of the greatest inventors in North Carolina history: James Henry Gatling and his slightly more famous younger brother Richard Jordan Gatling. In 1849, Richard was working as a store owner when he invented the screw propellor for steam vessels (though someone else also filed a patent for a similar propellor just hours before he did), a cotton thinner and a cotton stalk cutter. The cotton thinner and stalk cutter were instrumental in making the plantation more profitable. He also created a machine for planting rice, wheat and other crops, and he invented other agricultural machines that played a part in the mechanization of the United States.

But Henry was a prolific inventor as well. For years, he put his mind to a way to develop human flight. In fact, he took to the sky almost a generation before the Wright brothers. He tested his flying machine in the summer of 1873. Unfortunately, it crashed within its first one hundred feet of flight. Henry broke his leg, and he subsequently abandoned the project. So, the Wright brothers' flying machine was the first to log a successful flight. And the rest, as they say, is history.

However, five years earlier, Richard moved to the Midwest, where he created his most famous invention: the Gatling gun. His invention was a machine gun with a revolving cluster of barrels. He felt that the innovation would revolutionize warfare by allowing one man to do the same amount of battle duty of many once it was introduced in the 1860s. But the weapon was not as readily embraced as he had hoped until almost the end of the Civil War.

But on a more personal level, tragedy struck. And as is sometimes the way of things, the tragic death of Henry Gatling on September 2, 1879, was just the beginning of a macabre chain of events. Henry was murdered by a deranged local man. He was first shot in the face with a shotgun. When the attacker saw that Henry still alive, he clubbed him to death with a blunt object. The attack took place early one morning near Henry's hog pen. But there seemed to be a black cloud hanging over Gatling Farms after Henry's death, because three more deaths occurred in a relatively short period. First, a worker was fatally cut by saws in a cotton gin; next, the son of the new plantation owner fell into a peanut picker; and finally, an intoxicated servant froze to death on the property late one night.

But the story doesn't stop there. Not too long after that final death, various workers on the farm reported being followed by a ghost that would sometimes touch them on the shoulder. But the hauntings didn't stop there. Among the stories told about the Gatling plantation are those of a possum hunter who heard Henry's voice in the cemetery. Another story says that Henry smashed a glass on a farm worker's head early one cold winter morning. But one story persists today. Even now, there are reports most nights of a spectral figure walking the path on the old plantation grounds that led to the main house. Locals say it could very well be Henry keeping watch over the old home place, making sure no further violence is visited on his family home.

THE SPIRITS OF MELROSE (101 EAST BROAD STREET)

This home stands proudly on East Broad Street, a sterling example of elegance and grace from a bygone era. The house was built by Congressman

William Hardee Murfree in 1805. Murfree became a member of the North Carolina General Assembly in 1805 and 1812 and was elected to the Thirteenth and Fourteenth Congresses, where he served from March 4, 1813, to March 3, 1817. The house itself is a majestic two-story, Federal-style brick dwelling with a gable roof and interior end chimneys. The Greek Revival–style wings were added in the mid-nineteenth century. It also boasts a tetrastyle portico supported by Ionic order columns and has a second-story semicircular balcony. But don't let the beautiful face of the house fool you. Its story is a sad one indeed, one that could very well be the source of nightmares.

Colonel James Madison Wynn, and his wife, Virginia Brown Wynn, put their personal stamp on Melrose during their time in the house after they purchased it from Congressman Murfree. Once again, the home was a shining example of style and elegance. The Wynn family had been one of the more prominent families in colonial North Carolina, and the colonel intended to uphold that tradition and family standard in their new home. The family was involved in farming, raising trotting horses and operating the Petty Shores Fishery. That being the case, they were a part of everyday life in their community. However, tragedy knows nothing of social class or age, and the Wynns were about to learn that fact. In 1879, the colonel and Mrs. Wynn's daughter Meta Ashburn Wynn died in the house. She was only ten years old. She was buried in the family cemetery. And near her resting place is an area with no gravestones that could be a small garden area—or something else.

But that was just the beginning of the family's tragic history. In the early 1900s, one of the Wynns' daughters (to this day, no one is sure which one) became pregnant. Was it the stable boy? The groundskeeper? No one knows. And the daughter did her best to keep the fact a secret. Her father was a stern man and a strict disciplinarian. So, such a scandal would have had disastrous repercussions for the daughter. She was afraid to tell anyone about her dilemma. So, in an effort to hide the pregnancy, she had her corsets cinched tighter and tighter to cover up what was becoming an obvious situation.

Near the end of her pregnancy, the daughter, her corset cinched to a more than uncomfortable level, could not catch her breath. She became lightheaded and fell down the stairs. The fall did not kill her at that time, but her condition was discovered. But shortly after the fall, she died, and since her pregnancy was so close to full term at that point, her child was delivered stillborn. The family was ashamed, but even in their grief and disappointment, they allowed the daughter to be buried in Southall Lawrence

Cemetery in an unmarked grave, near the family plot. She and the child were buried there, and to this day, no one knows her name. Her sisters, Jenny Brown Wynn and Maude Wynn Copson, were buried along the back fence, just beyond the colonel and Mrs. Wynn's graves.

Previous owners of the house Richard and Lavinia Vann (they restored the house in the 1960s) shared that they heard strange, unexplained noises in the house. In some cases, when family members were in the basement, they would hear the front door open and close as if someone had entered the house. But when they went upstairs to check, no one was there. A more recent owner of the Melrose said that her dog sometimes sensed a presence in the house. The dog would stop in its tracks and look at something in the room (something no one else could see) and then turn and run out of the room. Could it be Meta Ashburn Wynn or maybe her unnamed sister and the baby?

MURFREE/SMITH LAW OFFICE (MURFREESBORO HISTORIC DISTRICT)

Built by the Murfree family around 1800, the Murfree-Smith Law Office was used by William Hardee Murfree and, later, W.N.H. Smith. It has also served as a post office and school, and the basement has served as a jail. And while the building has been a witness to some of history's prouder moments (W.N.H. Smith, a former owner, was elected to the house of commons from Hertford County in 1840 and the U.S. House of Representatives in 1859 and attended President Abraham Lincoln's first inauguration), it has also been a witness to some of history's darkest days.

On August 23, 1831, Governor John Floyd received a hastily written note from Southampton County postmaster James Trezvant stating, "An insurrection of the slaves in that county had taken place, that several families had been massacred and that it would take a considerable military force to put them down." The event, which became known as Nat Turner's Rebellion, was one of the largest slave rebellions ever to take place in the United States. Nat Turner led the revolt in nearby Southampton County, Virginia. The revolt itself lasted for little more than a day, but many people died before the violence was ended.

In the aftermath of the revolt, an escaped enslaved man was killed, and his head was placed on a post near the law office as a warning against any further attempts at rebellion.

During the 1980s and 1990s, when the law office served as the Murfreesboro Historical Association gift shop, volunteers reported, with some frequency, hearing voices coming from the basement when no one else was there. And when the basement was rented out as an apartment, some of the tenants reported hearing men murmuring upstairs late at night. They also heard footsteps walking back and forth on the main floor, though there was no one else in the building.

BRADY C. JEFCOAT MUSEUM (201 WEST HIGH STREET)

In 1922, the building that is now the Brady C. Jefcoat Museum was established as a school. About forty years after the school was opened, Marjorie Riddick was teaching her ninth grade class when something odd happened. She was popular with her students and was fond of telling them stories about her family's haunted plantation home just north of town. One of Mrs. Riddick's former students talked about the day the "odd thing" happened: "She [Mrs. Riddick] thought they [ghosts] followed her to school. The door came open, and she turned to the door and said, 'You just turn around and go back home. These students are in class now.' In a minute, the door closed, and she went right back to teaching without missing a beat!"

In the 1990s, the staff of the Murfreesboro Historical Association learned that a collection of antique music boxes, photographs, old washing machines and other interesting Americana artifacts from the period between the 1850s and 1950s was available. The owner of the collection was an older, somewhat eccentric man named Brady C. Jefcoat, a former general contractor, plumber and electrician. And while the Smithsonian and the North Carolina Museum of History wanted part of the collection, its owner was insistent that the entire collection be preserved. Those familiar with the old man said he was obsessed with his collection, so much so that he established an endowment for it. When Jefcoat offered to give the full collection to the Murfreesboro Historical Association, it purchased and upgraded the former Murfreesboro High School building in order to provide a new home for the unprecedented artifacts.

The collection includes toasters, washing machines, irons, churns, music boxes, radios, phonographs, Daisy air rifles, mousetraps, maple syrup taps, beekeeping equipment, player pianos, organs, mounted animals, dairy equipment and an X-ray machine that was used by shoe stores to accurately

Who—or what—watches over the Americana-related artifacts in the Brady C. Jefcoat Museum? © *The Ghost Guild*.

measure children's feet. The more than eighteen thousand items on display fill the seventeen thousand square feet of display space. However, the story doesn't end there—not in a town as haunted as Murfreesboro. Even though the items have a new home and Mr. Jefcoat realized his dream of having his collection preserved intact, some people wonder if the eccentric collector is still overseeing his collection as he did in life.

Some wonder if some of the items he collected have amassed a sort of residual paranormal energy. A case in point: when photographing items in the collection, one item in particular stands out. The photograph shows what appears to be a crystal ball in which a face is reflected. Members of the Murfreesboro Historical Association have looked for an explanation. They have tried to replicate the phenomenon. They have been unsuccessful on both counts. Their next course of action was to call on the Ghost Guild of North Carolina to ask them to conduct an investigation. The results should be interesting.

DEATH AT PARKER'S FERRY (PARKER'S FERRY ROAD)

The day started as a trip to visit relatives in Roxobel, North Carolina, a town about twenty-three miles south of Murfreesboro. The family, set for a day of visiting, laughing, reminiscing and eating some good home cooking together in the tranquil little town, began their journey in Suffolk, Virginia. But their trip ended on a truly horrific note. On November 16, 1924, Berry Credit, Odell Smith, Sarah Pope, Maggie Smith, Essie Smith and Roberta Smith made the trip to Roxobel in a Ford Model T touring car, something of a luxury vehicle in the 1920s.

But that's where the story takes a horrifying turn. How did six Black family members in a luxury car end up dead at the bottom of the Meherrin River later that night? The question is as much a mystery today as it was one hundred years ago. What were six people doing at the ferry at 8:00 p.m., a time when the ferry was not in operation? How did the car manage to roll into the river, killing everyone inside? Why did they not follow their original route back home through Murfreesboro instead of heading toward the river? Will anyone ever know the answer?

THE MORGAN-MYRICK HOUSE (402 EAST BROAD STREET)

The two-story brick Federal-style home with the double chimneys has seen a lot of history and has more than a few secrets of its own. The home was originally built by James Morgan in 1805. In 1830, the prominent merchant moved his family to Texas (at that point, still part of Mexico). Years later, on August 18, 1857, Fannie Myrick Southall was born in the house and died when she was only thirty-four years old. But unlike the Morgan family, who moved from the house in 1830, Fannie decided to stay, even after death.

It is said by previous owners of the house that Fannie is a bit of a playful spirit. Evidently, when the house is dark and everything is still, Fannie will come to a bed and blow in the occupant's ear. Sometimes, she can be seen walking through the dining room. Other stories relate the fact that Thomas Wynns is said to have killed a Confederate soldier who was accused of desertion on the front lawn of the house. Some say that the spirit of the Confederate soldier can be seen near the large magnolia tree in the front yard.

10

FORT FISHER

Some of the soldiers tasked with guarding the North Carolina coastline during the Civil War are still at their post.

Fort Fisher at Kure Beach was a major defense point during the Civil War, despite its humble beginnings. It began as little more than several sand batteries, the theory being that the sand and earth would absorb the impact of bullets and other projectiles fired at the fort. However, for returning fire, the fort had fewer than two dozen guns. Out of its half-dozen large guns, only the two eight-inch Columbiads (cannons designed for long-distance fighting that could fire either shot or a fifty-pound projectile) were suitable for seacoast defense. And while the arrangement was somewhat effective, in July 1862, Colonel William Lamb began the process of expanding and reinforcing the fort. The earth, sand and wood complex appeared simple on the surface, but within two years, Fort Fisher was an effective asset that defended over a mile of coast, protected the city of Wilmington and made the Cape Fear River a safe haven for the blockade runners that kept General Lee's troops supplied.

The fort remained a major stronghold until the waning days of the war. January 1865 was to be the end of the fort's effectiveness, although a month earlier, around the middle of December, Fort Fisher seemed to be all but impenetrable. In a battle launched by Northern forces that lasted two days, the fort held. Although thirty men were lost, the advancing Union forces were repelled. Then on January 12, 1865, Union forces under the command of Major General Alfred Terry attacked the fort.

While his predecessor had attacked from the sea with little success, Major General Alfred Terry, in a coordinated ground and sea maneuver, unleashed a devastating onslaught. He began with a constant bombardment of the fort from fifty-six ships for over two days. Then eight thousand soldiers went ashore for a relentless wave of hand-to-hand combat. After the steady barrage of ordnance from the fifty-six ships, the ground assault proved to be too much for the exhausted Confederate troops. In a final stroke, Union troops fought their way into a strategic point along Shepherd Battery, and the Confederate soldiers were forced to fight them from behind the walls of Fort Fisher.

Three days into the fighting, Colonel Lamb was wounded (he survived but was forced to use crutches for years), and General William H.C. Whiting took command. The general is rumored to have told Colonel Lamb, "Lamb, my boy, I have come to share your fate. You and your garrison are to be sacrificed." During the battle, Whiting was also wounded and subsequently captured. Still, the Confederate troops did their best to stand their ground, but they would not succeed. After both sides experienced heavy casualties in the bloody battle, losing over 2,200 troops in all, the fort fell, and the Confederate forces surrendered. With the surrender of the troops at Fort Fisher, the city of Wilmington also came under Union control. And as a tragic footnote to the aftermath of the battle, General Whiting was sent north to a Union prison, where he died about three months later, a sad footnote to the legacy of Fort Fisher.

In many cases, this would have been the end of the fort's story, but Fort Fisher wasn't finished just yet. It was waiting, and it was patient. The fort was quiet until the early 1900s, and then, the site woke up, and the sightings began. The first revenant to make its presence known is called

Who walks the battlements and stands guard at Fort Fisher 150 years after its final battle? © *Kevin Chesson.*

the "Sentinel in the Woods." Park employees, tourists and other visitors have seen him standing vigil in the woods just north of the fort, possibly on the lookout for approaching enemy forces. But he is not the only specter watching over the fort.

It is not unusual for people to report seeing the ghost of General Whiting standing in the spot where he was shot, looking toward the sea, possibly lamenting the fact that he was unable to stave off the final blistering attack that brought down the mighty Fort Fisher. Equally present is the specter of Colonel Lamb himself. Tourists, employees and even some historical reenactors have seen the great man walking along some of the nearby trails, the various strategic points of the fort and even the entrance to the fort's museum.

PART II

NORTH CAROLINA: A PIRATE SANCTUARY IN A SEA OF TROUBLE

Pirates are often portrayed as the swashbuckling Robin Hoods of the seven seas, brash rogues who lived life on the edge, their exploits spawning countless tales of danger and adventure. Sailing under the Jolly Roger, the legends painted them to be rum-drinking, kiss-stealing rascals who went where they pleased, took what they wanted and did it all with a heart of gold. Even our current idea of who and what pirates were is based, in part, on Long John Silver from Robert Louis Stevenson's classic book *Treasure Island*. But history paints a very different picture of the larger-than-life characters we have come to know as pirates.

Pirates were active primarily from the 1600s through the 1700s, and the coast of North Carolina, particularly the Outer Banks, was an area favored by many pirates at that time. Because of its unguarded coastline and the fact that it had many hidden inlets and coves, the North Carolina coast was a perfect place for pirates to hide. Take the Ocracoke area for example. The small islands that border both the ocean and the sound were hidden by tall oceanside dunes. From such vantage points, pirate ships could stalk their victims, attack seemingly out of nowhere and make a quick getaway once their quarry was disabled and unloaded. And due to the fact that the Outer Banks was part of a major shipping route, there was no lack of prey for the enterprising pirate. In fact, North Carolina was, in some cases, simply a stop along the way from the Caribbean to large colonial ports like Philadelphia. But it was a profitable stop for pirates who knew the area or worked with other pirates who were more familiar with the region's shoals and other hiding places.

But it wasn't just the geographic location that made the North Carolina coast a pirate haven. The North Carolina government during the colonial era was relatively weak and corrupt. This combination made it relatively easy for pirates to bribe local officials and avoid prosecution. And like the people whom Robin Hood befriended through his practice of robbing from the rich and giving to the poor, some North Carolinians were sympathetic to pirates. They saw the pirates as a way to get back at the British government and the wealthy merchant class when they were otherwise powerless.

Ships left America and carried products, such as lumber, tobacco, rice and dried fish, to Britain. British ships, on the other hand, came to America or sent American ships back to the American colonies with textiles and manufactured goods. And since the American colonial population increased from about 250,000 in 1690 to 2.5 million in 1754, that meant more goods were needed, so there were more ships on the ocean and more opportunities for the pirates who were waiting to ambush their next victims. And while it is not a part of history to be proud of, from the 1600s to the early 1800s, enslaved people were exchanged for materials and goods. Many were exchanged for gold or British-manufactured products and then shipped to colonial depots, primarily Charleston, New Orleans, the Caribbean Islands and New York. There, captives were again sold or traded for cash or goods (sugar, tobacco and timber). But they did not always remain in the lives they had been so brutally forced to endure.

One of the more interesting facts about the pirates who sailed during this particular period is that it was quite possible the pirates on any given ship couldn't understand each other. At first, this sounds more than a little odd. But there is a very simple reason for the communication problems. Often, pirate crews were made up of sailors from many different nationalities. On any given ship, there could be English, Dutch, French and even African crew members. It was not unusual for formerly enslaved people from the Caribbean and North America to join a pirate crew rather than return to the life of slavery.

And pirate crews were more than happy to welcome formerly enslaved people on board and initiate them into the life of a pirate. In fact, a pirate ship was one of the few places a Black man could get power and money in the Western Hemisphere in the 1600s and 1700s. It is believed that about one-third of the pirates active during this period were formerly enslaved. In some cases, these men were given the worst jobs on the ship, but that was not necessarily the norm. Many captains created a standard of equality among their men, regardless of race. On these ships, Black pirates could vote, carry weapons and receive an equal share of the spoils, just like everyone else.

The phrase "show your true colors" also comes from the age of pirates. When the captain of a pirate ship had a victim in sight, the pirates would deceive other ships by sailing under false flags. This practice kept pirate ships from attracting undue suspicion. Then the other ships, thinking the pirates were actually friendly, sailed close to them. And before they knew what was happening, the supposedly "friendly" ship would open fire, and scores of pirates would board the ship and take control. Then after the attack, the pirates would lower their false flags and show their true colors.

And while the assumption is often made that pirate crews were made up entirely of men, there was no rule that said only men could operate on pirate ships. Even in the 1600s and 1700s, being a pirate was an equal opportunity "profession." And while we are more familiar with the stories of pirates like Blackbeard, Calico Jack and "Gentleman" Stede Bonnet, there were women active in the world of pirates, and they were as fierce as any man who ever walked the deck of a ship. For example, Anne Bonny and Mary Read were two of the most famous (and ferocious) women pirates in history. Anne Bonny was the illegitimate daughter of Irish lawyer William Cormac and one of his servants. In an effort to hide the affair, Cormac dressed Anne as a boy and claimed she was the child of a relative.

Still, when word of his infidelity became known, Cormac, Anne and the servant moved to Charleston. Cormac became a successful plantation owner and member of the community. But headstrong and impulsive Anne married a poor sailor named James Bonny in 1718. When she was kicked out of the house by her father, she went with Bonny to the Bahamas to find work. There, she took up with the pardoned pirate "Calico Jack" Rackham, deserted her husband and went to sea to live the life of a pirate.

Mary Read had a similar story. Mary had been dressed in boy's clothes and was raised as a boy. Later, even while she was married, Mary served as a soldier in Flanders. After her husband died, she signed up to work on a merchant ship bound for the West Indies. Around 1718, Mary Read also joined Rackham's crew and met Anne Bonny. Bonny and Read became close friends and, as the story is told, were the fiercest members of the crew. They were rough, tough, given to cussing and ready and more than willing to do anything their male counterparts did on the ship.

Then there was Jacquotte Delahaye. She was believed to have been born in Haiti around 1630. Her father was killed by the British navy, and her mother died in childbirth. Jacquotte Delahaye was poor, a product of a poor country and hard circumstances, so much so that she joined a pirate crew. But Jacquotte was a fast learner, and in her later years, she commanded a fleet of ships. And like her male counterpart Blackbeard, Jacquotte Delahaye's hair was hard to forget. Whereas Blackbeard would sometimes tie fuses in his beard and light them for effect, Jacquotte Delahaye

They sailed the ocean, kings of the seven seas. And centuries later, some of them still sail with their undead crews. © *Artem Kniaz*.

had eye-catching, flaming red hair. That coupled with the fact that she survived many dangerous encounters earned her the nickname "Back from the Dead Red."

But she is not the only pirate who had a reputation for "coming back from the dead." There is a famous pirate (no stranger to North Carolina waters) who also seems to have come back from the dead. The legendary Blackbeard, or Edward Teach, was hunted down by Lieutenant Robert Maynard. Maynard caught the pirate at Ocracoke Inlet off the coast of North Carolina on November 22, 1718, and during the ferocious battle that ensued, Maynard killed him. When the battle was over and Maynard examined Blackbeard's body, he noted that the pirate had been shot five times and cut (during a cutlass duel between Blackbeard and Maynard) about twenty times. Then Maynard had Blackbeard's head cut off and his body thrown overboard. But the story doesn't end there. Keep reading to find out just how restless the ghost of Blackbeard was—and still is.

11

BLACKBEARD

As frightening in death as he was in life.

Blackbeard—the name alone still causes a chill when spoken in the right circles. And although his real name was Edward Teach, the name Blackbeard became synonymous with the pirate life. In *Blackbeard: The Fiercest Pirate of Them All*, he was described as "a 'tall spare man' with a long black beard from which he took his name."

> *Before the battle, he would plait the beard into little pigtails, tie them with colored ribbons and twist some braids behind his ears. Immediately before battle he would light several long, slow-burning hemp cords and tuck them under his hat, allowing wisps of smoke to curl up around his face.*
>
> *He wore pistols, daggers and a cutlass in a belt about his waist. Across his chest he wore a sling that held three brace of pistols, all six primed, cocked and ready to fire.*

Prior to his life as a pirate, not much is known about Edward Teach. Charles Johnson, an eighteenth-century author, claimed Teach had been a sailor based out of Jamaica during the War of the Spanish Succession and that "he had often distinguished himself for his uncommon boldness and personal courage." It is likely that Teach had been educated during his early days in England and was able to write. In fact, on the day of his death, the pirate was carrying a letter addressed to him by the chief justice and secretary of the Province of Carolina.

But what caused Edward Teach, a possible privateer, to make the transition to become Blackbeard, the most feared pirate on the seven seas? Well, that's another mystery in his life. From what we know, Edward Teach joined the crew of Benjamin Hornigold in 1716. Soon thereafter, Hornigold put Teach in charge of a sloop he had captured. Teach was in charge of the ship with six guns and approximately seventy men. As the story is told, Teach and his quartermaster, William Howard, developed a strong taste for madeira wine. On September 29, 1717, they took the entire cargo of madeira wine from the *Betty* at Cape Charles, Virginia, before they sunk the ship with its remaining cargo.

On November 28, 1717, Teach attacked a French merchant vessel, *La Concorde*, off the coast of Saint Vincent, and in the course of the attack, he forced the captain to surrender. This ship had originally been owned by the English and had changed hands several times by 1717. Blackbeard renamed the ship *Queen Anne's Revenge* and equipped it with forty guns. Oddly enough, though his ship was formidable and he had the reputation of being fearsome and ruthless, there are no verified accounts of Blackbeard having ever murdered or harmed anyone.

Blackbeard pillaged ships from the Caribbean to the Carolinas. Blackbeard, in fact, had a residence called Blackbeard's Castle in the Caribbean. But North Carolina was the place he called home toward the end of his career.

In September 1718, Blackbeard hosted the largest gathering of pirates to ever assemble in North America. The gathering took place at what is now called Teach's Hole. It is located on the sound-side beach near Ocracoke Inlet. The pirates sang, danced, ate and downed barrels of rum. The party lasted for days and only ended when the food and rum ran out. That was to be Blackbeard's final celebration.

The governor of Virginia, Alexander Spotswood, sent Lieutenant Robert Maynard of the British Royal Navy to track down the notorious pirate and end his reign of terror on the high seas. On November 22, 1718, Maynard caught up with Blackbeard in a deep-water channel just off the shore of Springer's Point. The ensuing battle was a bloodbath by all accounts. In the end, Blackbeard took twenty-five wounds from bullets, a sword and a dagger before Maynard's cutlass slashed through his massive neck.

With the fighting over, Maynard tossed Blackbeard's body over the side of the vessel and hung his head from the bowsprit of his sloop. But the pirate king was not finished—not yet. According to legend, the surviving pirates watched in amazement as their captain's headless body swam around Maynard's ship, searching for his lost head.

Blackbeard's Castle on St. Thomas. Legend has it that Blackbeard used the tower as a lookout point. *From the author's collection.*

Teach's Hole, located just offshore of Ocracoke Island, is the location where the infamous pirate Blackbeard was surrounded and killed. Some say he still roams here. © *Cynthia Mccrary.*

Maynard sailed away from Teach's Hole and made his way to Bath, Williamsburg and then on to Hampton, Virginia. There, he impaled Blackbeard's head on a stake at the entrance to the harbor, a message to any pirates in the vicinity that their days of piracy were coming to an end.

12

STEDE BONNET, THE GENTLEMAN PIRATE

From a life of wealth to the deck of a pirate ship.

Stede Bonnet was born to wealth and privilege. He was a man of means, cultured and refined. But sometimes, that's not enough, and for Stede Bonnet, there had to be more to life. With that thought in mind, the wealthy son of the aristocracy adopted the life of a pirate. But he was unlike any other pirate the world at that time had ever seen. He was, well, peculiar. Other pirates didn't finance their own ships—they captured them. Also, other pirates didn't pay their crews. They waited until they plundered a ship and divided the spoils. And because of his peculiar ways and his high-class upbringing, Bonnet became known as "the gentleman pirate."

And while the most unusual pirate on the seven seas enjoyed the life of a pirate, he wasn't necessarily one of the better pirates. Still, when Bonnet was eventually captured, he and his crew were charged with piracy against thirteen ships as well as murder. And while he sailed out of Barbados and was active in the Charleston, South Carolina area, the thing that makes him "one of ours" is his affiliation with Blackbeard. During a run-in with a Spanish man-of-war, Bonnet was injured and made his way to Nassau, where he met Blackbeard.

Blackbeard and Bonnet became friends and decided to work together. Their arrangement was that Blackbeard would take command of Bonnet's crew while he recovered from his wounds. After that, Bonnet walked around the deck, looking like a pirate captain, while Blackbeard actually ran the ship. They kept this arrangement until around December 19, 1717, when the two went their separate ways. Not long after that, the two met again, and Bonnet's crew, extremely dissatisfied with their captain, left him to join Blackbeard. The pirate asked Bonnet to join him on his ship, where Blackbeard told him he would make a better "man of leisure" than a pirate.

From there, the pirates went to Topsail Island to rest and refit their ships. When the *Queen Anne's Revenge* ran aground at Topsail, Blackbeard put Bonnet in command of a sloop. Then the two pirates went to Bath (then the capital of North Carolina) and were offered pardons if they swore to give up the pirate life. Blackbeard left Bath, and Stede Bonnet stayed behind to make arrangements to become a privateer. When he returned to Topsail Island, he discovered that Blackbeard had sunk several of his ships, pillaged them, took most of the supplies onboard and sailed away. In other words, he was stranded, at least for a while.

Ultimately, Bonnet and his crew were captured in Sullivan's Island in 1718. William Rhett, a local merchant determined to rid his city of pirates, led the group who finally captured Bonnet and brought him to Charles Town. After being found guilty at trial, Bonnet and approximately thirty of his crewmembers were executed at the site of White Point Garden, and their bodies were thrown into the marsh. But the story doesn't end there.

Many of those wayward souls still linger at White Point. People have seen floating apparitions and heard bloodcurdling screams in the night. And if you stand near Water Street and look down, you can still see the faces of Stede Bonnet and the other executed pirates staring back from their watery graves.

PART III

SHIPS IN THE MOONLIGHT

No book about coastal ghosts would be complete without saying something about the ships that made life possible on the coast. Fishing boats, cargo ships, pleasure boats and even battleships are part of any coastal area's backbone—and history. Many are retired or scrapped when their days of usefulness are done. Maybe they were damaged beyond repair. Maybe they fell victim to neglect. But in most cases, they perform their tasks until their final useful day.

But there are those special cases. Take, for example, the story of the *Crissie White*. On January 11, 1886, Captain Jeb Collins and his men were in the fight of their lives. Just off the coast of North Carolina, the ship was trying desperately to reach the shore. But the weather was working against them. People on the shore could only watch in horror as the ship and its crew battled for their lives against a massive winter storm. Ice had frozen the rigging, so the men had to lower the sails. Plus, the icy deck was treacherous, so even trying to walk was dangerous.

Waves hammered the ship, and between the extreme cold and the relentless pounding of the sea, the ship began to flounder. The sailors' fingers and toes were frozen, so even holding on was almost impossible. Some were swept overboard. And the ones who remained watched in horror as the mainmast cracked under the vicious waves that crashed on deck. Then a monster wave broke the mast in half, and the debris punched a hole through the deck. While the battle between man and the elements raged, the storm was so bad that lifeboats couldn't be launched, and rescue boats couldn't leave the shore.

The ship dipped once, twice. The remainder of the mast broke with a crack like thunder and was driven through the deck and the hull, sealing the ship's fate. There were no survivors. But the ship sails on. Since the tragic demise of the *Crissie White*, people have seen the ill-fated ship. When the weather is rough and the waves are pounding the shore, they can see the *Crissie White* and its ghost crew battling the waves, as they have done for centuries.

But some ghost ships are not so obvious. Just south of Topsail Island, near Rich Inlet is a spot where a ghost ship waits. Fishermen and pleasure boaters alike have seen the phenomenon. Watch your marine radar unit closely. Many people have reported seeing an image that indicates the presence of a ship, yet the coast is completely clear, no ships in sight. Even so, the radar often shows the ghost ship pursuing boats for a while. Eventually, the mark fades. It's possible the ghost ship returns fully to the spectral realm.

But that's just the tip of the iceberg, so to speak. North Carolina has some of the most famous ghost ships and ghostly ship residents in the world. Come on. I'll show you.

13

GHOST FLEET OF THE OUTER BANKS

They have been the silent sentinels of the North Carolina coast
for over four hundred years.

They are the vanguard of the past, silent sentinels forever standing watch over the eastern coastline. For over four hundred years, they have kept their silent watch from Cape Henry, Virginia, to Cape Fear, North Carolina, and all along the Outer Banks. They are the Ghost Fleet of the Outer Banks, and their stories are as varied as the times from which they come. Schooners, freighters, frigates, cargo ships, fishing boats and ships of war, all eternally anchored to the bottom of the sea. Many of these unfortunate vessels met their untimely demise due to the storms and dense fog that are a part of life on the island.

Cape Hatteras is known for such forces of nature. It is here that the cold waters of the Labrador Current converge with the warm Gulf Stream waters. Such a collision of elements often results in fog, fierce storms, stronger-than-normal currents and even shifting sandbars. In some cases, the position of the shoreline itself can change due to the area's powerful storms and strong currents. In fact, Cape Hatteras is the point that protrudes the farthest southeast along the northeast–southwest line of the Atlantic coast of North America. Because of its location, it is virtually the highest-risk area for hurricanes and tropical storms along the entire East Coast.

It is also the site where the two great basins of the East Coast meet and two major Atlantic currents collide: the south-flowing, cold-water Labrador

Current and the north-flowing, warm-water Florida Current, or Gulf Stream. The collision of these two major currents creates turbulent waters and a large expanse of shallow sandbars extending up to fourteen miles offshore. These shoals are known as the Diamond Shoals.

Cape Hatteras can experience significant wind and/or water damage from tropical systems moving northward offshore, while other areas (like Wilmington, North Carolina, and Myrtle Beach, South Carolina, to the south and Norfolk and Virginia Beach, Virginia, to the north) experience minimal to no damage. The Cape Hatteras area is infamous for being frequently struck by hurricanes that move up the East Coast of the United States.

All of these conditions are the bane of a sailor's existence, and any of them can be deadly. For example, the *Henry*, the *Horacio* and the *Islington* all went down in the winter of 1820. The wreck of the steamship *Home*, which sailed into the teeth of a massive storm, was just one of the sixteen wrecks recorded in 1837. Grounded just three hundred feet from Ocracoke, the *Home* had only two life preservers on board. Over ninety people died in the surf as they tried to make their way to shore. The *Pulaski*, in 1838; the *Congress*, in 1842; and the French bark *Emilie*, in 1845, all fell victim to the shifting shoals off the Outer Banks. And over the centuries, the toll continued to mount.

But currents, storms, fog and shifting shorelines are not the only reasons some of these ships met with untimely ends. Many of the five hundred shipwrecks that occurred along the 155-mile stretch from Cape Henry to Cape Hatteras were the results of the violent nature of war. From the 1585 sinking of the British *Tiger* to the 1969 sinking of the fishing trawler *Oriental*, war has claimed its share of victims and relegated them to the ranks of the Ghost Fleet. The Civil War and both world wars took their toll on many vessels along North Carolina's coastline.

North Carolina's waters have claimed thousands of vessels and countless mariners, who lost a desperate struggle against the forces of war, piracy and nature. The rich maritime heritage of coastal North Carolina runs deep with a vast array of shipwrecks. While the area is well known for shipwrecks dating from the age of North American exploration to the present day, the most prominent collection of shipwrecks comes from World War II's Battle of the Atlantic.

In fact, in 1942, the region along the Outer Banks was known as Torpedo Alley because of the high number of attacks on Allied and commercial ships by German U-boats in World War II. On May 11, 1942, while on patrol

Even the powerful lighthouses along the North Carolina shore weren't enough to protect some of the ships that are now part of the Ghost Fleet. Ocracoke Lighthouse. © *Alex Grichenko.*

off the coast of North Carolina, the HMT *Bedfordshire* was torpedoed by a German submarine. All thirty-seven of the British sailors on board were killed. In all, over five thousand individuals (including many civilians and merchant sailors) lost their lives, and their legacies ended in the graveyard of the Atlantic, where they took their various places as part of the Ghost Fleet of the Outer Banks.

14

THE USS NORTH CAROLINA

*The most decorated battleship of World War II evidently
has some of the most dedicated sailors as well. They're still on duty.*

In a book of stories like this, it is not often you have such excellent, firsthand expert experience to draw from. So, settle back and get ready to tour the battleship *North Carolina* and meet some of its ghostly inhabitants. The ship itself was the lead ship of the *North Carolina* class of fast battleships, and it was the first vessel of its type built for the United States Navy. It was the most decorated battleship of World War II, and it was the job of the battleship and its crew of 2,400 to protect carriers during battle. The design of the ship increased the main battery from the original armament of twelve fourteen-inch (356-millimeter) guns in quadruple turrets to nine sixteen-inch (406-millimeter) guns in triple turrets. Its construction was begun in 1937 and completed in April 1941, before the United States entered World War II.

After the attack on Pearl Harbor, the *North Carolina* was transferred to the Pacific to strengthen the Allied forces during the Guadalcanal Campaign. The ship was part of the Battle of the Eastern Solomons on August 24 and August 25, 1942, where it shot down several Japanese aircraft. After being torpedoed (but not seriously damaged) and repaired, it returned to the campaign and continued to fight in the central Pacific, including in the Gilberts and Marshall Islands and the Mariana and Palau Islands, the Battle of the Philippine Sea and offensive operations in support of the Battles of Iwo Jima and Okinawa in 1945.

The *North Carolina* operated briefly off the East Coast in 1946 before being decommissioned the next year and placed in reserve. In 1960, instead of being dismantled and scrapped, the ship was saved due to the efforts of citizens who were involved in a campaign to preserve the vessel as a museum ship in North Carolina. Even children from across North Carolina sent in dimes to help save the battleship.

So, the battleship was saved from the breaker yard and brought to Wilmington, where it was designated a museum and World War II memorial. And that's where it sits now, a silent sentinel on the Cape Fear River, a reminder of the cost of war. But unlike many such ships, at the end of the day, when the tourists have gone to their hotels and to dinner and the staff has gone home, the ship is not quite empty. In October 2020, Danielle Wallace (Battleship North Carolina programs director), Nelson Nauss (executive director/cofounder of the Ghost Guild Inc.) and Jon Michael (investigator with the Ghost Guild Inc.) were part of a program on the haunted battleship presented at the North Carolina Museum of History.

Daniele Wallace told the gathered crowd about her first ghostly encounters on the ship.

> When you live in Wilmington, you hear the stories about the battleship being haunted, and I came on board thinking, "OK, I'm going to play along, and if people ask me, I'm going to say, 'Oh, yeah, it's haunted.'" And this is until I saw the ghosts myself. The first time, I was participating in an EFP session down in the sick bay area with my coworker Shelly, and we saw this dark blue, dark purple orb just hanging over this particular bed. And when I said to the gentleman, the lead investigator, to please take a picture of that area, he did so. And as soon as he pulled his camera out, it was gone.
>
> I hadn't said anything to Shelly, but she whispered to me, "Oh, I saw that, too." But that was the first time. The second time was when I saw the Shadow Man in the mess decks of the battleship. I was talking to someone late at night. We were getting ready for an event called Ghost Ship, which is where we turned the ship into a haunted house for Halloween. It was just me and one other gentleman on board. I was talking to him, and I could see over his shoulder the Shadow Man. Just sort of walked past, and after a few minutes, he walked back across. The thing about the battleship is that things are completely still and quiet at night. Things don't move around. Well, nothing except the Shadow Man.

Who—or what—roams the corridors of the most decorated battleship of World War II? ©
The Ghost Guild.

The battleship's reputation for being haunted has spread far beyond the
Tarheel State. A few years before Danielle's Shadow Man sighting, the ship
was the site of an event for a private group. Part of the event included an
opportunity for members to meet Jason Hawes and Grant Wilson from the
TV show *Ghost Hunters*. They flew in the night before the event and arranged
to meet Danielle on board the ship at about 10:00 p.m. There were no

cameras, no crew, just the three of them. Jason and Grant had heard stories about the haunted battleship and just wanted to experience it for themselves with no one else around.

A number of paranormal groups have investigated the ship, and Danielle says there are some similarities in many of the reports. "One is that people will get touched…like their hair may be pulled, and sometimes, ladies will get a little pat on their behind. And what I tend to say to that is, 'Well, they're sailors, so what can we expect?'"

Nauss was in the communications area of the ship. Wes, a regular on many investigations, was there and accounted for. "So, we were in this area, and we were doing an EVP recording, when all of a sudden, you hear this thing in the background. And what's interesting about this is this is not an EVP. It's not something that was just recorded on our recorders and that we didn't hear. This was audible. We both heard it with our own ears." When the clip plays, the words are very distinct: "There's no reason to hide from us."

"So, we heard this, and when we ended up going back to our home base, so to speak, and we ended up speaking with Cecil, who was the volunteer on the battleship who was with us that night. He actually told us that what we heard made perfect sense, because this is an area of the ship that would have been off limits. And so, what we hear in this, as we were just talking in the background, you hear this stern male voice that says, 'Get out.'"

No reason to hide from us. Get out.

But not all of their encounters were as unwelcoming as that one. Ghost Guild member Kelly had an interesting encounter in the brig.

The first time I investigated the brig at the USS North Carolina, *I remember walking in and getting this immediate sensation like I was being watched. It's very dark in that space, and the darkness was illuminated by a single blue light from my RemPod EMF detector* [a device designed to generate an electromagnetic field and detect fluctuations in the field]. *I placed the RemPod at the entrance of the brig, and then I walked down, and I sat by the last cell. For a while, I sat in silence, the RemPod was not going off, and I just wanted to notice what I was feeling. It felt like somebody hovering over me, just checking me out. After a while, I started asking questions. And since I was in the brig where the naughty battleship boys would have been placed, I said, "I like the bad boys. If you were a bad boy, can you light up my RemPod?"*

Sure enough, my RemPod starts flashing and making all kinds of noise. One thing I also like to do on investigations is I like to research the music from the time period. In this case, I chose a song, "Bei Mir Bist Du Schoen." It's a Yiddish song that was very popular in the late 1930s. In the United States, singers like the Andrews Sisters and Ella Fitzgerald sang it. So, I chose that song because I figured in the 1940s or when these boys would have been on the ship, they would have probably known it. So, I asked my spirit, "Would you like me to sing you a song?" And my RemPod lit up again.

I started singing. "Of all the boys I've known, and I've known some / Until I first met you, I was lonesome." And then I would stop, and I would say, "If you want me to keep going, light up my machine." And it would light up. At the end of the song, I said, "Now, if you really liked my singing, please light up my machine." And it lit up. Made me feel pretty good. So, I asked a few more questions, but the night was moving along, and so it was time for me to go. I said to the guy, "Hey, it's time for me to leave. If you want me to come back and visit you again sometime, can you light my machine up one last time?"

Sure enough, it lit up. But this time, after it lit up, I watched a ball of light come up out of the machine and shoot into the cell next to it. I had never seen anything like it. Needless to say, it was a fun investigation, and I'm pretty sure I have a new boyfriend.

Yes, the ship is pretty active. Pot lids bang and benches move in the mess hall. Bed springs creak in the sick bay almost on command. When investigators asked the entity that was making the springs creak if it could make the noise louder, the spirit complied with the sound of something hitting the bed springs hard. And this particular manifestation is one of the most significant in many ways, because a physical force had to make the bed springs move. But again, some of the most interesting manifestations are those you can see. Jon Michael had one of his favorite experiences on the battleship with a previous team. It happened in the wardroom.

So, the place that we were meeting was in the wardroom. And so, the person I was with at the time, Aaron Wadia, had decided to kinda go back early "cause not a lot was going on." And so, we went to the wardroom, and we were waiting for everybody else to meet there so we can go to the next areas or whatnot. As we were hanging out, I saw what I thought, at first, was someone else who was on the investigation, Beth of Grave Concerns Paranormal.... When you're in the wardroom, you have a door on your left, which is what we came through, and there's a door on your right.

This ship served its nation well. Some of its crew continues to serve, long after their deaths. © *Mike D. Tankosich.*

And when I saw Beth walk by the door on the right and, well, it wasn't Beth, I just saw something like in white, and she was wearing a white hoodie. That's why I thought Beth. And Aaron acknowledged it, too. It was kinda like—it's one of those things that you can tell when someone sees something. We're kinda sitting around. The rest of the team start showing up. I think Nick, who is also part of the Ghost Guild, asked if anyone had seen Beth, because Beth hadn't come up yet, right. And I was like, "Yeah, she's like right outside." You know, "I just saw her walk by." And we went out there, and no one's out there. And not only is no one out there, but the only way in or out that particular area was the door. So, that was weird. And so like, you know, unless it's like someone jumped over the side.

15

THE CARROLL A. DEERING

One of the most baffling disappearances in maritime history.

On January 29, 1921, the *Carroll A. Deering* was making a return trip to Hampton Roads, Virginia, from Barbados when it passed the Cape Lookout Lightship. According to the lightship keeper, the crew was milling about when a crewman, who did not look or act like an officer, reported that the ship had lost its anchors. The following day, the ship passed the SS *Lake Elon* southwest of the Diamond Shoals Lightship at approximately 5:45 p.m. The *Deering* seemed to be steering a peculiar course. This was the last report of the ill-fated *Deering* before it was found run aground and abandoned.

At 6:30 a.m. on January 31, C.P. Brady of the Cape Hatteras Coast Guard Station spotted a five-masted schooner in the morning light, run aground and helpless on the shoals. It was reported that the ship's decks were awash, its sails were set and its lifeboats were missing; it appeared abandoned. Due to heavy seas, the surf boats failed to reach the wreck. Finally, the wrecker *Rescue* arrived on the morning of February 4 and, with the cutter *Manning*, reached the battered ship around 9:30 a.m. Captain James Carlson of the *Rescue* boarded the ship and confirmed its identity as the *Carroll A. Deering*. After an investigation of the ship, it was discovered that all personal belongings, key navigational equipment, certain papers and the ship's anchors were missing. Furthermore, food was laid out as if in preparation for a meal. But there was no sign of the crew.

In January 1921, everyone on the *Carroll A. Deering* disappeared—103 years later, their fate is still a mystery. *Public domain.*

Even the Library of Congress, in its *Headlines and Heroes* publication, has questions about the ill-fated voyage and few answers.

*In April 1921 a message in a bottle found by a man on the North Carolina coast seemed to give the answer to the mystery. "*Deering *captured by oil-burning boat," the note read. The State Department began an investigation into the* Deering *and several other missing ships, and it was suspected that the* Deering *had been captured by pirates. Then newspapers began reporting the possibility of a Bolshevik plot to steal the ships, cargo and crews and somehow whisk them all away to Russian ports.*

By September, however, it was discovered that the message found in the bottle, the only real evidence of what may have happened to the Deering*'s crew, was in fact written by the man who supposedly found it. Mr. Christopher Columbus Gray faked the note in the hopes that he could discredit the staff at the Cape Hatteras lighthouse and take someone's job, it was reported. The hoax had prompted investigations by the U.S. Navy, Treasury, State Department, Department of Commerce, and Department of Justice. Without the note, however, the investigations fizzled out and ended without an official explanation.*

As speculation sailed through the pages of newspapers and government investigations, comparisons were made to other mysterious nautical disappearances. Still within recent memory for many was the disappearance three years earlier of the USS Cyclops *along with all passengers and crew—nearly 300 people had gone missing. The* Cyclops, *a 19,000 collier took a similar route to the* Deering—*departure from Brazil, a stop in Barbados, and then up the U.S. coast. The ship left on March 4, 1918 on a trip that should have taken no more than 9 days. Could it have been sunk by a German ship as a part of hostilities in the First World War? Again, no evidence was ever found to provide us with answers.*

In a similar fashion, the SS *Hewitt*, a steel-hulled bulk freighter, left fully loaded from Sabine Pass, Port Arthur, Texas, on January 20, 1921. It was bound for Portland, Maine, with a stop in Boston, Massachusetts. It made its regular radio calls on January 24 and January 25 and reported nothing unusual. It was last seen 250 nautical miles (460 kilometers) north of Jupiter Inlet, Florida, at which point, the ship and its entire crew disappeared without a trace.

The Library of Congress's *Headlines and Heroes* asks, "What did the *Carroll A. Deering*, USS *Cyclops* and the *Hewitt* have in common? In addition to the missing people, they all passed over that mysterious stretch of ocean known as the Bermuda Triangle. Myths about the Bermuda Triangle wouldn't start until some forty years later, but the ghost ship *Carroll A. Deering* is still discussed as one of its many mysteries."

What we know for sure is that the wrecked and battered hull of the *Deering* was all that was left to signify the vessel's strange passage. In March 1921, as the vessel began breaking apart on the shoals, it was towed away and then dynamited. The ongoing lure of the *Deering* mystery may be due to the many historical threads uncovered in the investigation of this amazing story. Agent Thompson of the FBI visited Dare County in July 1921. Among the leads he followed were stories of Bolshevik-sympathizing pirates, rum-running gangsters and mutinous sailors. When he asked local coast guardsmen about the theory that the crew had mutinied and abandoned ship before striking the shoals, they responded, "Impossible!" The coast was too rough for lifeboat landings. In the end, the investigation proved fruitless. No trace of the crew, the ship's log or the navigation equipment was ever discovered.

16

The Flaming Ship of Ocracoke

Was this ship the vehicle of revenge for its dead passengers and crew?

The plan to escort German and Swiss refugees from England to the American colony of New Bern in the 1600s had an innocent enough beginning. But like many an ocean tale, somewhere along the way, something went very wrong. Toward the end of the journey, things took a tragic and otherworldly turn.

In the late seventeenth and early eighteenth centuries, religious wars raged throughout Europe, and one of the results was a mass exit of people most effected by the war, including people in what is now Germany and Switzerland. Because of their Protestant faith and faithful adherence to their religious beliefs, such devout people became prime targets for those who wanted to abolish certain religious practices. When James II ascended to the English throne in 1685, there was already great tension between the nation's Catholics and Protestants, as well as the monarchy and Parliament. From the outset, James made enemies due to his support of freedom of worship for Catholics and his decision to go as far as to appoint Catholic officers in the army.

Through his Declaration of Indulgence, many of the penal laws used against Catholics were suspended, and some Protestant dissenters were even granted immunity. Late in 1687, he dissolved the existing Parliament and attempted to create a new Parliament that would support his decisions. In addition to his unpopular decisions, many of his subjects saw his relationship with the French as a potential political problem. By this time, there was talk of a revolt, and the king's fate was sealed. In 1689, James II was forced to abdicate the throne by Parliament. His daughter, Mary (who was next in the line of succession), and her husband, William of Orange, were brought in to replace the unpopular James II. Now, with a German king on the throne, many English alliances began to change. And with this change, William was happy to use the army he now commanded to expand the wars he had already been fighting in the regions of modern-day Germany and Switzerland.

The resulting escalation of the war created a massive number of refugees who were being driven from their various homelands. As the situation worsened, the new king and queen of England accepted thousands of these refugees. For a time, there was a steady stream of displaced German and Swiss immigrants who took refuge in England. The fact that many of the refugees were craftsmen and skilled tradesmen was a mixed blessing. There was now an abundance of workers who were ready and willing to take on projects for a lower price. This was good news for the community at large but not so much for the existing workers and tradesmen. Their work was no longer in demand, and the jobs were fewer and farther between. The local craftsmen had never known such a lack of work, and tensions began to rise.

In answer to the growing labor issue, Cristoph von Graffnreid, a Swiss baron, offered a solution. He would escort a large number of these refugees to a settlement called New Bern in the Carolina colonies. The king and queen agreed that this would be a fine solution, and plans were made to begin sending the German and Swiss refugees to New Bern. For the most part, the German and Swiss travelers were happy and excited about this new turn of events. And this is where the story takes a tragic turn.

Whereas most of the crossings were undertaken in safety and without incident, one ship in particular was anything but safe. It set sail during the time of the new moon in September. And unfortunately for the passengers, the captain of this particular ship was a greedy man, a dangerous man. As the passengers were boarding the ship, he noticed that this particular group was carrying more gold and jewels than many of the groups he had carried to the Carolinas. These items were the refugees' family treasures, items of great sentimental and monetary value brought from their various homelands which they were now taking to their new homes in New Bern. But the greedy captain had other plans.

On a dark and moonless night, as the ship drew closer to the Outer Banks of North Carolina, the captain and his bloodthirsty crew crept below decks and, one by one, slit the throat of each passenger while they slept. And once they were sure every passenger was dead, the crew loaded the treasure on the ship's longboat. Then, to make sure nobody discovered their crime, the crew poured oil on the decks and set the ship on fire.

As the ship caught fire and flames roared against the night sky, the captain and his crew rowed the longboat toward the town of Bath, a notorious pirate gathering place. As they made their way to their hideout, the pirates laughed about the plight of the now dead travelers and gloated about what they had just done and how rich they were going to be. But something wasn't right. Amid their depraved revelry, the captain turned and looked behind them. And the sight he beheld made his blood run cold. The doomed ship was moving. The sails were flaming tatters, and there was no wind, but the ship was speeding toward them as though it was at full sail. But the ship was not being steered by human hands, because every person on it had been killed in their sleep.

The captain cried out that what they were seeing was not possible. Still, the flaming ship, filled with the dead, continued to speed toward them. No matter what the crew did, the ship followed them, drawing ever closer until it was right on top of them. As the pirates screamed, the flaming ship rammed the longboat, sending it, the treasure and the murderers to the bottom of the sea. The next day, the burned-out ship washed ashore on Ocracoke. And now, over three hundred years later, it is said if you scan the horizon off Ocracoke Island on the night of the new moon in September, you might just see the outline of a flaming ship manned by an undead crew making its way silently toward the island.

PART IV

TALES OF THE UNEXPLAINED AND THE MACABRE

In a book titled *Haunted North Carolina Coast*, you certainly expect to read about specters in graveyards, ghosts in houses, shadowy shapes lurking along dark pathways and long-dead soldiers walking along the battlements of a Civil War fort. And every such tale will include landmarks and anomalies that stand as silent reminders of tragedies and supernatural events, like the hoofprints in Bath that mark the tragic yet somehow fitting end to a boisterous bully's final race.

Then there are the houses and other buildings where the supernatural is almost a way of life, where otherworldly entities interact in an effort to make themselves known in our world. Thalian Hall, almost the entire town of Murfreesboro and the Burgwin-Wright House are just a few of the places where spirits from the supernatural realm have taken up residence—or maybe they can't leave.

There are the spectral ships that appear out of the mist and the fog on certain nights, their ghostly crews replaying some pivotal event. There is the battleship *North Carolina*. It served with honor, was rescued from the scrap pile and now, in its rest, plays host to a number of sailors who, even after death, just never left.

And while these are all supernatural in nature, that in itself gives us an explanation of sorts. Nell Cropsey still "lives" in the house that was her home on the day she died a century ago. Maybe she is waiting for her final justice. In the swamp, an old woman still searches for her lost son long after her own life ended. They are all supernatural, but they all have some sort of ingrained logic.

From mysterious lights to monuments that cry, some things in this world simply defy explanation. © *sunburntblogger.*

But now we come to the other stories, the ones in which no tale precedes the event. There is no story of a murder victim seeking revenge or a long-dead pirate still searching for his head. No, the stories that follow are not so easily explained. Some are chilling, some are a little funny and some are just perplexing. There may be no rhyme or reason as to why they these events occur or why these stories ever happened in the first place, but they are all things that, as Arsenio Hall used to say on his television show, make you say "Hmmmmm."

17

THEODOSIA BURR

Her disappearance is still one of our country's greatest unsolved mysteries.

Theodosia Burr Alston was one of America's first women known for her learning and mental capability. She was widely acknowledged to be intelligent, cultured and sophisticated. She was also the daughter of Vice President Aaron Burr, and the various scandals associated with his name and his exile weighed heavily on her. The circumstances surrounding her father and her own resulting unhappiness were most likely major factors in her subsequent health issues and depression. Her disappearance and the mysterious appearance of her portrait in a home on the Outer Banks remain some of the most intriguing unsolved mysteries of the first days of the America.

In 1801, Theodosia Burr was married to Joseph Alston, a wealthy South Carolina planter and later governor of the state. Far from being the culmination of a young woman's dreams, this marriage was not a happy one. It was, in fact, a marriage more of economics than a promise of love between a husband and wife. Aaron Burr is said to have offered his beautiful daughter to the wealthy South Carolinian to provide some security for his declining family fortune. Burr may have also been looking for a way to align himself with powerful allies. In 1807, Burr was put on trial for treason. His plan was to lead many of the southern states in a secession. If successful, he would be installed as the king of the new country, which included the states involved in the plan and parts of Mexico.

After a trial rife with controversies and questions about executive privilege and state secrets privilege, Burr was ultimately acquitted. Chief Justice John Marshall could find no solid evidence of treason. His reasoning was that the intention to divide the country was not in itself an act of treason. He wrote: "A combination or conspiracy to levy war against the United States is not treason, unless combined with an attempt to carry such combination or conspiracy into execution; some actual force or violence must be used in pursuance of such design to levy war....There must be an actual assembling of men for the treasonable purpose, to constitute a levying of war."

Immediately following Burr's acquittal, straw effigies of Burr, Marshall and other prominent participants in the trial were burned by angry mobs. With such actions taking place and any and all political capital he may have once had now gone, Burr fled the country. Despite the acquittal, the vice president fled to Europe for four years in a self-imposed exile to avoid further scandal. He would not return to New York until 1812.

Both father and daughter were devoted to each other. In August 1809, she wrote to him, "You appear to me so superior, so elevated above all other men." At the time of Burr's return, Theodosia was severely depressed. For years, she had suffered long bouts of illness, which made her physically weak. She was also deeply grieving the recent death of her young son. Months passed before the grief-stricken Theodosia was well enough to travel to New York to see her recently returned father.

In South Carolina, Theodosia Burr Alston suffered from long bouts of ill health. She frequently traveled to spas seeking treatment and would often withdraw from social life in Columbia and Charleston for months on end. Dr. David Hosack's letter to Joseph Alston on June 12, 1808, said, in part,

When she arrived she was much exhausted by the fatigue of her voyages—added to the diseases under which she labors—but by change of climate I hope she is likely to be benefited—her appetite tho [sic] still bad is somewhat improved—the pain on her right side and shoulder still continue troublesome, attended occasionally with violent spasms of the stomach and her other complaints....Her general appearance is somewhat improved. My attentions hitherto have been directed to the general state of her health, when that is mended she will be enabled to make use of such remedies as are calculated to remove her local diseases—with the views of improving her strength.

I have advised her to pass a few weeks at the Ballston Springs—she has already made some use of the waters and finds them to agree with

her—but drinking them at the springs will be more serviceable to her—they are especially calculated to improve her appetite and strength....Yesterday she left New York on her way to the springs—should any thing [sic] of importance occur and I receive information of it, you may expect again to her from me.

By August 20, Theodosia's health had improved to the point that she was able to try some of the remedies the doctor had suggested to her husband. In addition, he recommended two to three baths per week as a way to alleviate some of her discomfort. By the fall of 1812, Theodosia yearned to be reunited with Burr, despite her ill health. Her husband, Joseph Alston, had reservations about the timing of such a dangerous trip, especially since he was unable to accompany his wife on the voyage. As brigadier general of the state militia and the newly elected governor of South Carolina, he could not leave the state while the War of 1812 was underway.

The disappearance of Theodosia Burr Alston remains unsolved to this day. *Portrait courtesy of Walpole Library in Farmington, Connecticut.*

In January 1813, just seven months after the death of her son, Theodosia was aboard the ship *Patriot* when her story took a macabre twist. The ship disappeared off the coast of Cape Hatteras on its way to New York. The Library of Congress's *Headlines and Heroes* picks up the story here.

Travelling by sea during wartime was risky as British warships were patrolling the Atlantic Coast. Severe weather was also a concern in addition to the threat of pirates who were active in Carolina waters. Plans were made to try and safeguard Theodosia's travel. Burr persuaded an old friend and business associate, Dr. Timothy Greene, to accompany his daughter on the journey. Alston chose the vessel Patriot *for the trip because of its reputation for excellence and speed. After saying goodbye to her husband at Georgetown on December 31, 1812, Theodosia, the* Patriot *and all aboard disappeared and were never seen again. After weeks passed without word of her safe arrival in New York, her concerned father and husband began to fear the worst.*

Burr and Alston chose to believe that Theodosia had met her death by drowning after a severe storm sunk the Patriot. *However, as word of the disaster filtered through news channels, a stream of rumors and stories emerged about her mysterious fate and the conjecture would continue for decades. Many speculated that the* Patriot *fell victim to pirates who trolled the Outer Banks. Over the years, several deathbed confessions from aged or imprisoned pirates were reported in newspapers. In 1820, two men who would be executed for other crimes, confessed to plundering and sinking the* Patriot, *killing all onboard. In 1833, a man described in detail how he forced Theodosia to walk the plank.*

Other stories claimed that she had been held captive in Bermuda by one pirate who made her his mistress, or that she was murdered resisting the advances of a pirate while captured by famed privateer Jean Lafitte. More fanciful tales include everything from her wedding ring thrown in a bottle at sea to an Indian chief in possession of a gold locket inscribed with her name. She has also been linked to the mysterious "Female Stranger," who is anonymously buried at St. Paul's Episcopal burying ground in Alexandria, VA.

But the mystery deepens even more at this point. In 1869, Dr. William Pool was visiting Nags Head when he was given a portrait of an unknown woman by a local resident in partial payment for his medical services. The woman who gave the portrait to Dr. Poole said it had survived a shipwreck that occurred in the area more than fifty years prior. One of the doctor's relatives later photographed the portrait and sent it to some of the Burr family members. They compared the portrait to a surviving engraving of Alston. After a careful comparison, they said the portrait was definitely that of Theodosia Burr Alston, although the identity of the artist remains a mystery.

18

BATH'S CURSE

An evangelist, infuriated by a town's indifference, cursed the town of Bath.
Some say the curse is still in effect.

George Whitefield, an evangelist credited with being the catalyst for the Great Awakening, a major revival that swept the East Coast in the 1730s and 1740s, was a British preacher with a powerful voice that easily carried over massive outdoor crowds. In addition to his work in the colonies, he was one of the founders of Methodism and the evangelical movement. Instead of accepting a church and serving as the senior pastor, Reverend Whitefield chose the life of an itinerant preacher, and in 1740, he traveled to North America, where he preached a series of revivals. And while he was cross-eyed and had a strong cockney accent, Whitefield drew crowds in excess of eight thousand, some to hear the gospel and others because they had never seen anything like the odd-but-famous preacher.

While Whitefield was generally well received, his methods were often seen as controversial, and in many cases, he found himself debating with (and disputing) members of the local clergy. His tour through many of the thirteen colonies included the North Carolina towns of New Bern and Bath. He visited New Bern twice, once in 1739 and again in 1764. The first time, he was a bit upset, predominantly angered by the minister's son taking dancing lessons. He wrote in his journal that, while the people were "uncommonly attentive…melted to tears," he still "mourned much in spirit, to see in what indifferent matter everything was carried on." But while the

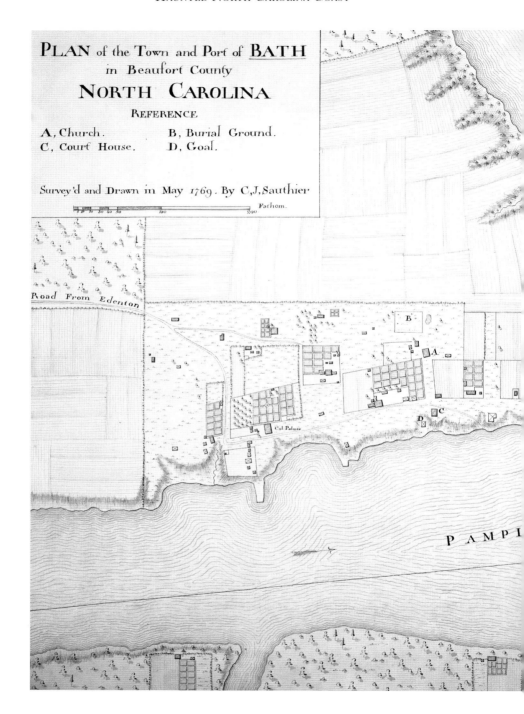

PLAN of the Town and Port of **BATH**
in Beaufort County

NORTH CAROLINA

REFERENCE

A, Church.   B, Burial Ground.
C, Court House.   D, Goal.

Survey'd and Drawn in May 1769. By C,J,Sauthier

Fathom.

Road From Edenton

Col. Palmer

B

A

D C

PAMPI

"Map Survey'd and Drawn in May 1769 by C.J. Sauthier"; date of publication: 1769; former owner: George III, king of Great Britain (1738–1820). © *British Library Commons.*

evangelist's opinion of New Bern was less than positive, his feelings about the town of Bath were much less charitable. Bath was, at that time, on its way to becoming a major sea port, but Whitefield considered Bath a den of iniquity, a veritable Sodom and Gomorrah of the modern world.

Whitefield was upset with Bath's laid-back, live-as-you-please attitude and the fact that it offered protection to many of the pirates of the day. In fact, Edward Teach, better known as Blackbeard, lived in Bath after he was pardoned by the governor. With that information in mind, he arrived with plans to shake up the town and force it into a state of holiness, as he had done in so many other towns. But there was a problem with his plan: the town of Bath was happy with itself just the way it was and had no desire to change. That knowledge infuriated Whitefield.

The passage he used as an "exit strategy" came from Jesus's instructions to his apostles when encountering those who will not listen. "As you enter the house, greet it. If the house is worthy, let your peace come upon it; but if it is not worthy, let your peace return to you. If anyone will not welcome you or listen to your words, shake the dust off your feet as you leave that town," (Matthew 12:12–14, NRSV).

It is important to understand that, with all his accomplishments, Whitefield was, as one might say, a real piece of work. Along with his appearance and odd speaking voice, everywhere George Whitefield traveled, he carried a coffin with him, and he slept in it every night. His public statement about the casket implied he wasn't afraid of death, and he challenged the crowds to have the same assurance about their salvation. But it has also been said that he slept in his own coffin at night to avoid the revelry of the local inns.

But the locals of Bath were having none of it, and they made their displeasure with the traveling preacher well known. They told him in no uncertain terms that he'd put that coffin to good use if he stayed. And Whitefield, who had never had that kind of reception, was livid. He raised his fist and said, "If a place won't listen to The Word, you shake the dust of the town off your feet, and the town shall be cursed. I have put a curse on this town for a hundred years."

Whitefield is said to have taken off his shoes, banged them together, and said, "I say to the village of Bath, village you shall remain, now and forever, forgotten by men and nations until such time as it pleases God to turn the light of His countenance again upon you." And with those words, he left. But that's not the end of the story. Soon after Whitefield's departure, the town of Little Washington was established down the river. Its location

Left: Bath was poised to be a successful port until George Whitefield cursed the town. *Work titled* Whitfield preaching in Moorfields AD 1743, *by Eyre Crowe.*

Below: St. Thomas Episcopal Church in Bath is the oldest church in the state. © *Lei Xu.*

made it a more natural port, and the town grew, whereas Bath did not. Still, Bath remains a charming town filled with historic sites, including North Carolina's first library, the state's oldest existing church and tales of history's most feared pirate, Blackbeard. Its population as of today is 245.

19

THE LOST COLONY

How does an entire settlement disappear?
And what is the significance of "Croatoan"?

In the late 1500s, the English made their first attempts to settle in North America. Sir Walter Raleigh sent 120 settlers to establish a colony on behalf of Queen Elizabeth I. The trip from England to the New World took three months. The settlers arrived on Roanoke Island, one of the barrier islands located just off the coast of North Carolina, on July 4, 1584, and soon established relationships with two Native tribes, the Secotans and the Croatoans. But by April 1586, many of the settlers had returned to England due to a shortage of food and a series of Native attacks.

On July 22, 1587, John White and 115 new colonists returned to try to establish a second colony in the area. Their first act after landing was to check on the previous colony. To their surprise, they found nothing but a skeleton that may have been the remains of one of the English garrisons. Still, they formed a second colony on Roanoke Island. Later that year, John White, the leader of the colony, headed back to England to get more supplies, and during that trip, a major naval war broke out between England and Spain.

Queen Elizabeth I immediately called on every available ship to confront the Spanish Armada. So, it would be three long years before John White could return to the colony, his wife, his daughter and his granddaughter, Virginia Dare, the first English child born in the colonies. When he

The Lost Colony. English Explorers read "Croatoan" on a tree here in 1876. *State Archives of North Carolina.*

returned in 1590, the settlement was deserted. The settlers had mysteriously disappeared. There was absolutely no sign of the colony—no people, no dwellings, not a single possession.

The only clue he found was the word "Croatoan" carved in a tree. Croatoan was the name of an island south of Roanoke that was home to a Native tribe of the same name. It was the same tribe the settlers of the previous colony had established a relationship with. A hurricane prevented White from pursuing this lead, and the colonists were never found. Investigations into the fate of the "Lost Colony" of Roanoke have continued over the centuries, but no one has come up with a satisfactory answer.

But the mystery doesn't stop there. As the legend is told, after White headed back to England, Wanchese, who had visited England with White, launched an attack against the colonists. When the attack was over, there were few survivors. Three of the survivors were Ananias and Eleanor Dare and their daughter, Virginia.

Manteo, another Native who had visited England with John White, rescued the family. Tragically, the little girl's parents died, so Manteo's tribe took Virginia in. They changed her name to Winona and raised her as one of their own. As she grew, she was said to be very beautiful and knowledgeable in the ways of the forest.

A gravestone commemorating the Lost Colony. What happened to every man, woman and child in the colony? © *Joe Sohm.*

A white doe. A bride to be. A tragic symbol of love. © *Pawel Strykowski.*

When she became of age, she had many suitors within the tribe. She chose a handsome brave named Okisko. Unfortunately, in doing so, she rejected the tribe's medicine man. His name was Chico. The choice of Okisko infuriated the old medicine man, and he vowed that if he couldn't have Winona, nobody could. When Winona did not relent, the medicine man transformed her into a beautiful white doe. The beautiful animal was often glimpsed in the forest or standing at the edge of the water, as if waiting for someone.

Heartbroken, Okisko sought the help of a medicine man from another tribe at Lake Mattamuskeet, about seventy miles away. The brave found Wenaudon, one of Cisco's rivals, and told him the story of the white doe. Wenaudon felt compassion for the young brave and crafted an arrow with a magic oyster shell tip. He told Okisko that if he aimed true and pierced the heart of the doe with the arrow, she would turn back into the woman he loved. Armed with that knowledge and a new hope, he returned home.

Shortly after he arrived home, Wanchese ordered a hunt for the white deer. He said the doe had eluded his hunters long enough. So, Okisko joined the hunt armed with his magic arrow. After a few days, he spotted the white doe in the forest at the water's edge. He knocked his arrow and waited for a clear shot. When the doe turned, he saw his chance and released his arrow. The shot was straight and true. Unfortunately, Wanchese had shot his silver arrow, presented to him during his trip to England, and both arrows pierced the doe's heart.

A gray mist covered the doe, and Okisko ran to it. When the mist cleared, he saw that it was Virginia Dare, whom he knew as Winona, lying on the ground. But his heart broke completely when he realized two arrows had pierced her heart and that the silver arrow had killed the woman he loved. Through a haze of tears, the brave wrapped his love in a cloak and buried her in the center of the settlement on Roanoke Island, which had been abandoned years earlier.

20

CEDAR GROVE CEMETERY'S WEEPING ARCH

Can the arch actually predict who will be the next to die?

There, among the Spanish moss and crumbling gravestones, stands an arch, a silent sentinel that has overseen countless burials since it was erected in the mid-nineteenth century. The massive, triple-arched gateway to the Queen Street entrance of Cedar Grove Cemetery in New Bern is a true spectacle. It is made of coquina, also known as "shell stone." The calcite has a soft gray color, derived from the millions of mollusk shells that form the material. The arch was constructed in an

What makes the archway weep as a funeral procession enters the cemetery? And if a teardrop lands on you, are you the next to die? © *Lei Xu.*

era when many cemeteries were being refurbished, and impressive (even opulent) entrances were becoming more common with each passing year.

Soon, however, the citizens of New Bern began to notice that the arch was more than just a spectacular entrance to the place where generations of local families were laid to rest. Not long after the arch was constructed, people noticed that water dripped from the archway. This didn't happen all the time, only when a funeral procession passed through the arch. Sometimes, the water was clear, and sometimes, it had a reddish tint. But it only dripped during funeral processions.

Often, people would comment on how much the water looked like tears. Some even observed that, often, when drops of water splashed on someone as they passed under the arch, that person was the next to die. What causes the arch to weep as the dearly departed pass beneath it? And what causes the red tint on some occasions and not others? And is it true that the arch has a way of predicting who will be the next to die? Should you have the opportunity to pass under the arch, take an umbrella—just in case.

21

THE GRAY MAN OF HATTERAS

There are some things you don't want to see on a walk along the beach.

Hurricanes are a way of life on Hatteras Island. The island is uniquely positioned to catch the brunt of bad weather. The worst weather normally comes between June 1 and November 30. Although severe weather can come any time during the year, the strongest storms typically impact the North Carolina coast between mid-August and September. Cape Hatteras is very close to the Gulf Stream, and that allows hurricanes to strengthen due to warmer ocean temperatures during the summer. Also, Hatteras's physical location means hurricanes that might miss other parts of the East Coast tend to impact the island.

So, between its geographic location, the Gulf Stream and the fact that Cape Hatteras receives wave activity from almost every storm that affects the Atlantic coast, Hatteras is a prime target for hurricanes, tropical storms, nor'easters and other severe storms. As such, the locals are very familiar with the National Weather Service, NOAA and other severe weather tracking agencies. But there is another source that tells them exactly how bad a storm will be. He's the Gray Man, and he's never wrong.

Often seen walking in the shadow of the Cape Hatteras Lighthouse or in other areas along the shore, the Gray Man's presence is a warning that bad weather is approaching. He is an indistinct, nondescript figure who normally arrives with the first light winds of a storm. Never a presence in minor weather systems, the appearance of the Gray Man means the island

Above: Who—or what—is the Gray Man? © *Dentramper Tramp.*

Left: The Gray Man can often be seen in the shadow of the Cape Hatteras Lighthouse just before a storm. © *Yulia Ivanova.*

is in for a rough time. It's best to keep your distance, however. Witnesses say if you approach him, he will disappear.

Who is this mysterious Gray Man of Hatteras? Some say he is the spirit of someone who was terrorized by a storm, and though he didn't survive, he stays to warn others, so they won't share his tragic fate. Others say he is a ghost, a sailor originally from the island who comes back to warn others about impending storms. And still others say he was never a man at all. He's not human. He's not a ghost or a spirit. He's a force of nature, generated by the storm itself. But whatever he is, it's always best to heed his warning.

22

DYMOND CITY LIGHTS

Some towns never die.

Dymond City was never a large town, but it was comfortable. It was located on Highway 171, about ten miles from Jamesville. Dymond City was what was known back then as a company town. Its houses were owned by company, the workers paid their rent to the company and everyone did their shopping at the company store. By 1885, the town had a hotel, a school and houses for the workers and families. And while the town had a good twenty-five years, the old-growth timber was soon depleted. Add to that the fact that a second railroad line was built nearby, and the Jamesville and Washington Railroad and Lumber Company went out of business.

Not long after the demise of the railroad and the lumber business, the town began to dwindle. The company tore up the tracks and sold the land, so the entity that had provided a living for the town's citizens was officially gone. By 1920, the post office was closed, and in 1927, the town caught fire. Its houses, hotel and everything else was burned, and within a few years, the forest finished the job. The town of Dymond City was no more—at least not in the way it once existed.

The road leading to what was once Dymond City comes to an intersection. One side is gated, and the other side, the side where people see things, is not. But what exactly is it that those people see? Often, people report seeing lights bobbing up and down in the woods. Sometimes, they see a fireball

What's out there where the town used to be? Ghosts? Spectral railroad men still at their post? The memory of a town? © *Ilkin Guliyev.*

moving above the trees. But what are they? Some say they are the ghosts of railroad men faithfully manning their posts from a railroad that went away one hundred years ago. Some say it is the people of the former Dymond City who can't or won't leave their home. What do you think it is?

23

THE COTTON EXCHANGE

Everybody needs a gathering place, even the undead.

Often, when a place is said to be haunted, there is a story or a tragic event that provides us with an "ah-ha" moment and makes everything fall into place. So, why are the sounds of phantom footsteps on the hardwood floors and strange shadows that defy description so commonplace in the Cotton Exchange? And what about one of the Cotton Exchange's more permanent residents, the specter called Fred? For 150 years, he has appeared at night wearing all black, his long, curly hair moved by unseen currents. And rather than being a benign spirit, content to watch the world of the living walk by, he is often known to stop behind shop patrons and breathe down their necks. Then, ghostly purposes fulfilled, he vanishes into the surrounding gloom.

Is there something about the building that attracts the various ghosts and specters that haunt its shops and walkways? It's hard to tell. The building had a start similar to that of hundreds of others just like it around the country. Originally used by Alexander Sprunt as the base for his successful cotton export business in the early 1900s, the exchange was where cotton farmers brought their crop to be sold to buyers and traders, who then sold the cotton to manufacturers around the world. There's nothing too sinister there. The building's barbershop, laundry service and wholesale grocer of that bygone era have all been replaced with boutique shops. Its architecture has been preserved. And the Cotton Exchange is now one of the more popular tourist destinations in Wilmington.

And it is not just for the living. Aside from Fred, one of the more visible spectral occupants of the exchange is known as the Lady in the White Dress. It is not unusual to see her almost anywhere in the Cotton Exchange, but most often, she is seen in one of two places. In the German Café, she is most often seen at the top of the steps in the upper dining room. She also manifests on the stairs in Fidler's Gallery. One particular story surrounding the specter says a little boy asked his mother if she believed in ghosts. "I don't know. Why do you ask?" she answered her son. "Well, when I was in the bathroom, there was a lady in there. Then, all of a sudden, she wasn't."

In addition to the Lady in the White Dress, there are other ghostly visitors who make themselves known at the exchange. Men and women in Victorian clothes have a tendency to make themselves known and then vanish. Men in morning coats and women in long dresses walk by the former location of the Fire and Spice Gourmet Shop on a regular basis, only to vanish from sight. And a ghost dressed in a suit and top hat is evidently a music lover. He can normally be seen standing at the listening station near Golden Gallery.

However, not all of the ghosts, specters and apparitions are content to watch as you walk by, appear and then disappear or silently go about their ghostly business. Some of them are a little more "hands on." Take

It looks festive enough, but something draws spirits to the former cotton exchange. © *Zimmytws/Tom Schmucker.*

the soldier, for example. Most often, he can be seen around the Port City Pottery location. He looks every inch the soldier in his blue uniform with a gold braid. He's quite impressive. Oddly enough, he seems to appear only to people who can see and hear him. And he is not shy about making his wishes known. He wants to talk, to be heard. It's really sort of sad. As the story is told, he asked one patron of the exchange, "Why do people keep walking by me? I just want to tell my story to someone."

Then there are the two little girls. Now, these two are a handful. They enjoy playing pranks, and their handiwork is hard to miss. The spirit of one little girl remains primarily in Top Toad. She goes through the store knocking over displays and unplugging various items. She can leave the shop a real mess. Her counterpart makes her presence known at the Scoop. Often, she will pour syrup on the counter, push stacks of plates over and play with the wind chimes. She has also been known to turn the microwave, blender, radio and mixer on and off. The young girls have also been known to speak, but their soft voices are lost in the crowd noise.

But that brings us back to the question: Why? What attracts the undead to the Cotton Exchange? Granted, Wilmington has a history like those of most other American towns. Slavery, murder, corruption and injustice are as much a part of this town's history as its selfless and giving residents who have upheld the common good and fairness. So, nothing about the location seems like the kind of thing that would make it hard for these specters to pass on after their deaths. But whatever the attraction, the nineteenth-century brick building is one of Wilmington's most famous paranormal locations.

24

THE GREAT DISMAL SWAMP

There's something not quite right out in the swamp.

The Great Dismal Swamp is the largest remaining swamp in the United States. It lies in the upper northeast corner of North Carolina, on the state's border with Virginia. Comprising 113,000 acres, it is a fraction of its original 1 million acres, but the swamp has seen a lot of history—and other things. As the American colonies began to expand, Native communities fled to the swamp for refuge. And prior to the Civil War, many enslaved people took to the swamp to flee slavery. From the late seventeenth century to the end of the Civil War, thousands of people called maroons (runaways who occupied remote and uninhabited regions) lived in relative secrecy throughout the swamp. They saw the inhospitable area as a step up from their former lives.

But from such inhospitable areas come tales of the mysterious and the macabre. One story includes a graveyard in the swamp. It appears only to people who have lost their way in the swamp. Explorers who search for the graveyard have never found it. And interestingly enough, the graveyard has been "found" in a number of locations, not one static place. But that shouldn't be surprising. Many hunters who have tracked deer and bear in the swamp tell stories of game that has vanished. Deer and bears that were shot in the course of hunting trips were said to have disappeared without a trace. No telltale hair or blood splatter can be found in the vicinity where the animal went down. They simply vanished.

The Great Dismal Swamp is an inhospitable land of mysteries. © *Crystal Dawn Venters.*

The swamp has spawned many stories about specters encountered in it. One such story is that of a Native love gone tragically wrong. Two lovers approached their wedding day with great joy. But tragedy struck when the bride to be died on the morning of the wedding. She was buried in the swamp, and her young future husband was so overcome with grief that he swore to anyone who would listen he could see her paddling across Lake Drummond in a white canoe. His grief became so great that he fashioned a raft and went out on the lake to find her. As he followed his spectral bride to be, he drowned in the lake. Now, the two lovers can be seen paddling together in a white canoe.

This ghost, known as the Lady of the Lake, was the inspiration for Edgar Allan Poe's poem "The Lake," and the swamp was the inspiration for Irish poet Thomas Moore's "A Ballad: The Lake of the Dismal Swamp." In addition, the swamp was used as the setting for Harriet Beecher Stowe's book *Dred: A Tale of the Dismal Swamp*. And in one case, the swamp could have played a more tragic part in the literature world. Robert Frost, heartbroken when he was rejected by Elinor White, visited Lake Drummond (located at the center of the swamp) in the height of his depression. He once told a biographer that he'd hoped to lose himself somewhere in the swamp's wild landscape and never return.

Oddly enough, despite the fact that many people have gone into the swamp and never come out again, no bodies have ever been discovered in or recovered from the swamp. On one hand, it is possible that the acidity of the water disintegrates the bones of anyone or anything left behind. But maybe that's just another mystery of the Great Dismal Swamp.

Bibliography

American Hauntings. "Dead Women Do Tell Tales: The Lingering Ghost of Nell Cropsey." https://www.americanhauntingsink.com/nell-cropsey.

Cape Fear Unearthed. "If Ghosts Should Walk in Thalian Hall," ep. 5. October 31, 2019. Wilmington, NC: StarNews Media. https://omny.fm/shows/cape-fear-unearthed/if-ghosts-should-walk-in-thalian-hall.

CarolinaBeach.com. "Fort Fisher State Historic Site." https://www.carolinabeach.com/fort-fisher.html.

CoastalGuide.com. "Ghost of Fort Fisher." https://www.coastalguide.com/ghost-of-fort-fisher.html.

Colonial Ghosts. "The Great Dismal Swamp." August 15, 2017. https://colonialghosts.com/the-great-dismal-swamp/.

Cotten, S.S. *The White Doe; The Fate of Virginia Dare; An Indian Legend.* Philadelphia, PA: J.B. Lippincott Company, 1901. Retrieved from the Library of Congress. https://www.loc.gov/item/01031845/.

Farah's Simple World. "Haunted Cotton Exchange | Wilmington NC | The Cotton Exchange Shops | Hanted Place in Wilmington NC." August 15, 2022. https://www.youtube.com/watch?v=rz8hF5OsSfs.

Ghosts, Legends, and Lore of Historic Murfreesboro Tour

Goldburg, Johanna. "Dr. David Hosack, Physician to Hamilton and Burr." January 21, 2016. https://nyamcenterforhistory.org/tag/theodosia-burr-alston/.

HauntedHouses.com. "Wilmington, North Carolina: Thalian Hall." http://hauntedhouses.com/north-carolina/thalian-hall/.

Hushed Up History. "With a Casket and a Curse: George Whitfield and the Town of Bath." January 30, 2022. https://husheduphistory.com/post/674865519657172992/with-a-casket-and-a-curse-george-whitefield-and.

Library of Congress. Chronicling America. https://chroniclingamerica.loc.gov.

North Carolina Department of Natural and Cultural Resources. "Blackbeard: 'The Fiercest Pirate of Them All.'" June 9, 2011. https://www.dncr.nc.gov/blog/2011/06/09/blackbeard-fiercest-pirate-them-all.

North Carolina Digital Collections. https://digital.ncdcr.gov/.

North Carolina Ghost Guild. Video Presentation, NC Museum of History Program on the USS *North Carolina*.

North Carolina Ghosts. https://northcarolinaghosts.com.

Preik, Brooks Newton. *Haunted Wilmington and the Cape Fear Coast*. N.p.: Banks Channel Books, 1995.

Price, Mark. "'Ghost Ship' with a Cat—But No Crew—Wrecked on Outer Banks 100 Years Ago This Week." *News and Observer*, January 31, 2021. https://www.newsobserver.com/news/state/north-carolina/article248873154.html.

Rankin, Dorothy, and Lee Lowrimore. "The History and Construction of Thalian Hall." *Wrightsville Beach*. https://wrightsvillebeachmagazine.com/the-history-and-construction-of-thalian-hall/.

Roberts, Nancy. *Ghosts from the Coast*. Chapel Hill: University of North Carolina Press, 2001.

Sprunt, James. *Chronicles of the Cape Fear River 1660–1916*. 2nd ed. Raleigh, NC: Edwards and Broughton Printing Company, 1916.

Thomas, Heather. "The Unsolved Mystery of Aaron Burr's Daughter." Library of Congress Blogs. *Headlines and Heroes*. January 22, 2019. https://blogs.loc.gov/headlinesandheroes/2019/01/the-unsolved-mystery-of-aaron-burrs-daughter/.

Virginia Paranormal. "Dymond City Road—Haunted Roads and Bridges." May 13, 2019. https://www.youtube.com/watch?v=HcP07R3jsBY.

Wikipedia. "Burgwin-Wright House." https://en.wikipedia.org/wiki/Burgwin-Wright_House.

———. "Stede Bonnet: Resumption of Pirate Command." https://en.wikipedia.org/wiki/Stede_Bonnet#:~:text=Bonnet%20this%20clearance.-,Resumption%20of%20pirate%20command,their%20supplies%2C%20before%20sailing%20away.

ABOUT THE AUTHOR

Thomas is an award-winning writer, essayist, playwright, reporter, TV news producer and a three-time American Christian Writers Association Writer of the Year. He has been a joke writer for the late Joan Rivers, and his horror novel, *Something Stirs*, was one of the first haunted house novels written for the Christian market. He is also the only writer to have been included in writing projects with Reverend Rick Warren and Stephen King in the same week. He even lived in a haunted house in Georgia for two years.

FREE eBOOK OFFER

Scan the QR code below, enter your e-mail address and get our original Haunted America compilation eBook delivered straight to your inbox for free.

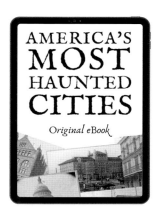

ABOUT THE BOOK

Every city, town, parish, community and school has their own paranormal history. Whether they are spirits caught in the Bardo, ancestors checking on their descendants, restless souls sending a message or simply spectral troublemakers, ghosts have been part of the human tradition from the beginning of time.

In this book, we feature a collection of stories from five of America's most haunted cities: Baltimore, Chicago, Galveston, New Orleans and Washington, D.C.

SCAN TO GET
AMERICA'S MOST HAUNTED CITIES

Having trouble scanning? Go to:
biz.arcadiapublishing.com/americas-most-haunted-cities

Visit us at
www.historypress.com